Everest A. Byrns
#44
For the love
of the game

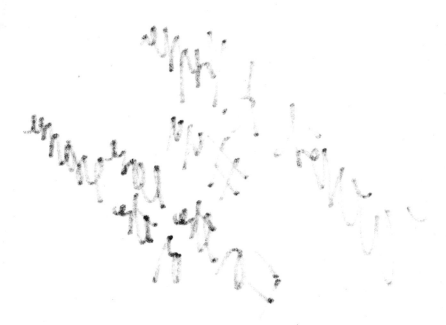

Everybody Fumbles

by
Earnest Byner

Earnestbyner21.com
EB 21 Production
Second Printing
© 2015

Everybody Fumbles
Table of Contents

• • • • • • •
Foreword by Jimmy Raye

It surprises me that such an essential thing as character has stopped being taught along with athletic pursuits. I've seen athletes succeed on the field without it. Many athletes' disappointment can be attributed to an absence of personal qualities of character. Seemingly successful individuals don't lose the personal qualities of character? As athletes and coaches learn the technique for accumulating earthly treasures, they can lose the real meaning of living well and doing good things.

If you define success to narrowly, you can succeed beyond your wildest dreams while losing the things that are essential to being successful: family, friends, loved ones and spiritual identify, thus leaving only personal tragedy.

I try to keep this in my heart always in my most important work, being a man. My players-former and present have their own lives, their own paths to follow as they move on in the world. But none are likely to duplicate my path. They will have different fights. The most valuable things I can give them are the simple meaningful example of trust and love. Character will equip to build good lives.

The author of this book, Earnest Byner, displayed confidence, fortitude, pride, persistence, fearlessness, and focus, the true treasures of the spirit that can get past defeat, such as the fumble in one of the biggest games and moments in a very successful career. The strength of his convictions and character leaves a valuable legacy.

Everybody Fumbles is a testament to over coming adversity and helping others. We both know ambition to achieve something for love and family, the drive to be successful is in this blue print. I'm hopeful and sure you will agree after reading this review.

Jimmy Raye
NFL Coach

· · · · · · ·

Acknowledgment

Byner didn't join in the celebrating in the locker room after the game Sunday. He left quickly to go out to dinner with his wife, Tina. During the game, he looked at her in the stands and they pumped their fists at each other.

"She's been there for me since the eighth grade. She knows me better probably than I know myself, to tell you the truth," he said.

I want to thank my wife for always being there for me.

I love you...

THANKS! For our four beautiful, strong and courageous children:

Semeria, Adriana, Brandi, Kyara...

My heart...My soul...

· · · · · · ·

My immediate family oldest to youngest:
Granny (Evelyn Dixon Reeves) MA (Bernice Reeves Bailey),
Brother-Willie B. Collins, Sister-Angela Collins Reid (Leek),
BRO-Roderick Byner, Baby Sis-Chevelle Byner Logan

· · · · · · ·

Acknowledgement of childhood competitors and friends and coaches:
Carl Cummings, Mackarthur and Calvin Reeves, Tim Hill, Joey,
James Edwards, Tommy Lee, Thomas, Rosco & Leroy Hall, Dog Man,
Bo Peep, Henry Taylor, Scott Blizzarrd, Herman Driskell Jr, Jeff and
Mike Miller. Coaches: Morris, Bentley, Smith, Whitten, Rev. Horace Ray.

Thanks for giving me the foundation.
I'm sorry if I left someone off the list. Concussions.

EB

· · · · · · ·

Introduction

There are different layers to an onion or cabbage. As you peel back the most obvious there is another one presented. You peel back until you get to the core.

Everybody Fumbles has many layers. Of course it's about the fumble that happened in the AFC Championship game in Denver and other aspects of my life as a kid, in high school, college and the NFL. Enjoy the stories associated and transfer the lessons to other aspects of life.

EB

PS - At points in the book there are lines drawn for the reader. They are there for notes, thoughts or discussion points.

Life Philosophy

· · · · · · ·

Everybody Fumbles

"It seems like for my whole career, I've heard that we need somebody faster, younger, someone with fresh legs," Byner said. "It's always we need somebody better than Earnest Byner. I have nothing to prove. If you come out every day with something to prove as your motivation, you're a somewhat shallow individual. I come out here every day to work for this football team."

It's a crucial time in the game. We are driving as we have been all day. There has been some exciting play all day long. We have dug ourselves a hole in the first half WITH TWO FUMBLES AND ONE INTERCEPTION. We were Down 21-3 after the first half, but now we are driving for a score to tie the game. I've run a passing play to the back of the end zone and jogged back to the huddle. After that play, I had to pick up a blitzing linebacker while barely being able to stand. Now... I'm in condition but still breathing hard as we go to the LOS. Bernie had called 45 TRAP. I'm handed the ball coming down hill to get in back hip relationship with my pulling guard (DAN FIKE). The play is designed to get inside, but the tight end has collapsed the end man of the line of scrimmage. The guard bounces, so I bounce. I take a look outside and see 85 running off but decide to get vertical..... I'm scoring! They haven't stopped me all day and not now but.....

Well damn! I'm on the ground without the ball. Dead tired and exhausted while knowing I've let my guys down. What a way to end this comeback. I fumbled and caused us NOT to tie the game. After all we had gone through to get there, I! The leader, the workhorse at that time, did what was unthinkable.

Where has this happened before? Have I not made mistakes before? Were there any mistakes early in the game on both sides of the ball? Have there not been any made prior to then? Have you not made any mistakes? Truth is...this was mine at the height of fame and on one of the grandest stages and in one of the best games every played. IT WAS ONE OF MY BEST GAMES EVER!

I have come to believe that the experiences that you have gone through prepare you for the experiences that are to come. But this?! This was a life changing or life killing moment. How can I deal with this? Where is my strength? Where is my protector at this time?

After the game I answered the questions, got the support by everyone from Mr. Art Modell to Big Daddy Carl Hairston. For the most part I was left alone. QUIETNESS! No one ever said ...TO ME... you cost us! Well not on the team. Even when our plane had to abort the take off and we went into the airport to the bar. We took shots of crown to deaden the pain. The letters of support were nice! The words of the people that said I took their dream away were heart felt and understood while they stung.

I squarely put the loss of the 1987 AFC CHAMPIONSHIP GAME on my shoulders. I've finally had the nerve to look at it in its entirety and saw a number of plays that cost us a chance to win. All that played in the game on both teams made mistakes and plays that were not titled.

EVERYBODY FUMBLES on some level, whether it's in the public light and gets major press or it's in the privacy of your car, house, classroom or gym. My mistake was blasted to the heavens and served to be motivation for others and me. I was able to recover and grow while using that experience to help others. My energy was forever changed.

I was initially hurt, disappointed, and driven to get back to where we were. So many people talked about me and continued to feel like they had to say "DON'T FUMBLE" whenever the opportunity was presented. It made me become self-conscious. I became more and more paranoid regarding it. What are people thinking, what will they say next and what can I do to keep anyone from saying anything? It became a struggle for me to go out and be comfortable. I began to feel like I was being watched. It consistently ate at me and made me weaker in almost all aspects of my life. What I once attempted to master, I began to only try to survive. As with other times when I had to resort to assisting others to take the onions off of me. Understanding that we all will struggle at some point gave me strength, because I knew I could help someone else, especially after I had my key life lesson.

How will you use yours? For if it hasn't happened to you yet, then you better hold your butt, cause it's coming. Use it, accept it and teach from it because everybody does Fumble.

The blame for the loss has to be placed on someone. The goat is what they call the player that makes the mistake or should I say the key mistake that can cost the team the game. Some coaches or other teammates, family members and the media want to blame someone for the loss. Now, the reality is that at one point everyone on a team will make a mistake. Each mistake can cause the team to lose the game. As we know, there seems to be one or two errors that are and will be the focus of the next day's news. It may even be the topic in the locker room and or in the coaches meetings.

Hopefully you won't be constantly reminded of the mistake that you make. Hopefully you will learn from it and then use it to assist and teach others. Even if you are constantly reminded of it, still Love yourself and others enough to continue to pursue your dream.

Notes:

_____

_____

_____

_____

_____

_____

_____

_____

_____

_____

_____

_____

_____

_____

•••••••
Culture Change

Straight from the Coach

I was a coach from Earnest Byner's rookie year through 1988 at the Cleveland Browns. He was a dynamic force from his rookie year well past that to the end of his career. I'll speak about my experiences and opinions only...

He was a player we needed to put into the lineup even as a rookie. As a rookie, he made up a personal group called "Ernie's Group" which was composed of some tough guys who would thrash around and cause havoc in a game. We weren't a very tough offense in Cleveland at the time. Then there was a coaching change and Earnest became a starter along with Kevin Mack. Of course they both gained 1000 yards for only the 3rd time in NFL history. We were playing the Jets the last game of that season and found out during the 4th Quarter, Earnest needed just a few yards. We called 38 Snatch Crack, a sweep around the right end to get his 1000.

We made the playoffs and lost to the Dolphins. Earnest lit it up with well over 100 yards using Power O. The Cleveland Browns were a divided team prior to that season - offense vs. defense. Offense had to ride on their own bus because the defense somewhat bullied the "soft" offense. It was true and the coaching/scouting staffs were trying to change that culture without much luck. Along came Earnest as a starter with a fierce attitude and a sense of entitlement to share in the team. He boldly got onto the defense bus and declared, "There'll be no more offense vs defense". He stood up and the Browns became one. He changed the culture! He would openly call out his teammates if they didn't perform with toughness and perseverance.

Back to the Dolphins loss in the playoffs. We went to Dodger Town on Vero Beach, Florida to practice for the playoff game. On Wednesday during our team drills, he called out lineman who missed their backside blocks and was running over his own teammates so much we pulled him out of the next day's drills for fear of him hurting one of our own players.

He made us a TEAM. He WILLED our team to never give up, play at a high level all the time and not tolerate mediocrity or selfishness. Earnest epitomized the phrase "Say what you do and do what you say".

We became an electric team, making the playoffs. Then came "The Fumble" which has been immortalized. Lindy Infante, the offensive coordinator asked for a play, and I suggested 45 trap. It worked with a giant hole. Earnest had an easy path to the goal line, which would have put us into the lead with little time, left. Oops, our receiver loafed on the play and his DB just happened to turn around and inadvertently stuck his arm out as he was swinging his body around. It punched the ball out and they recovered.

One of our guys was lazy and the Broncos dumbed into the fumble and the Super Bowl trip.

It was crushing to the Browns. What was even sadder were the moments on our sideline. There on the bench sat Earnest Byner all by himself with his head in his lap lamenting what had just happened. I noticed him and felt so much empathy for his loss. I couldn't help myself, so I went and sat beside him, put my arm around him and told him that we wouldn't have been there without him. "You have meant everything to what we have become as a team". The joy of victory and agony of defeat were captured in those moments. I still feel the pain for Earnest because his spirit didn't deserve that. He meant so much to so many during his playing time in the NFL!!!!

I love you Earnest Byner,
Howard Mudd

Notes:

_____

_____

_____

_____

_____

_____

_____

_____

_____

_____

· · · · · · ·
Acceptance

While sitting on the sideline watching the Broncos take a safety, after the fumble, the process of dealing had began.

It's near the end of 1987 AFC Championship Football Game. So, I'm sitting on the sideline on my helmet waiting for the game to be over. Bernie had walked down to me and stood by me. WEBSTER came over to offer a word. We patted each other. I don't remember anyone else or anything else. I'm thinking that losing was not even a consideration. We had a good game plan and we were riding that play off zone as a team.

Exhaustion and total deflation were MY FEELINGS. I had given all that I had. I ran pass routes, run blocked for Kevin Mack and pass block for Bernie Kosar. I remember going on the field for another play. I believe it was a hell Mary, well Hail Mary pass. After the play, I remember Gary Kubiac coming up to me to shake my hand. He told me I was a great player.

I remember getting into the locker room. Mr. Modell was there. He gave me a hug and some words of support. After a while I was hustled off to the media room for the press conference.

The only thing on my mind was I had given all I had on the field. That was my focus. I could not talk about anything OTHER than how I had played. I considered no other plays that happened nor other players. It was my fault that we lost.

Now to me that was always the case. Not just in this game, in all the games I played, my play was the determining factor. It was how I prepared, thought and played. No! No one told me to feel or think that way. It was just the way I was driven. It gave me direction and purpose.

So, I didn't try to explain away all that had happen or try to speak for the team other than to say I played as hard as I could and left it all on the field. Someone asked me about Buckner, but I had no idea who they were talking about. However, later in my life, I saw a ball go through his legs on first base and understood that he was the only player that made a mistake in that game. He was blamed for losing their championship. I'm sure that there were others that were interviewed. I don't know if anyone else felt like they had cost us the game. I just knew I had to stand and man up.

If you ever have to be in front of the media after a hard loss, I feel, the best way to handle it is to be totally honest regarding your play. Sometimes you may feel you can't face it, but do because eventually you will have to. It was a struggle, but I never thought of not talking or pointing the finger other than at myself.

Notes:

Earnest wins first place at the age of 9 in a sports competition.

• • • • • • •

From the Beginning

Success came to me early and often in all athletics.

Lying in the cornfield kicking and screaming for what seemed like days was my response to my very first pinched nerve in football. I was maybe seven or eight years old. My task was to hike the ball to the quarterback, to my big brother, then run a deep post route to get open. The snap count was on two. My brother said "hut" and the young man over me jammed my neck back into my shoulders. Dang!

Football has always been there for me. I always played whether it was out back in the cornfield or in front of my grandmother's house in West End, a little section of Milledgeville, Georgia.

Initially, I got into the game because of the enjoyment it brought to me, my brothers and the neighborhood kids. We all progressed on to play in some park leagues.

Eventually we got into sports for the local schools. Each of those brought a different level of competition, coaching, and eventually personal growth.

When I first went out to play football, the coach started me at the offensive line position. He had me at guard. We ran a drill where I had to pull around the right side. I did. Yes! The coach saw something and shortly thereafter I was in the backfield. It didn't matter to me where I played. I was playing football.

I played running back until I got into the eighth grade. We had a bunch of good runners, so the head coach decided to play me at quarterback and run an option offense. That way he had all his best players on the field. Again, no problem cause I loved playing the game, so it did not matter where I played. (My best friend from middle school was one of the backs Larry "DUCK" Simmons... still miss you man). We kicked a whole lot of booty with that team.

As I progressed into high school, college and the pros that basic love for the game never ceased. Even at the end of my career, I was still happy to get on the field. It didn't matter if it was a third down play, where we needed a conversion or a special teams play blocking for one of the young returners. I loved it.

Notes:

_____

_____

_____

•••••••
Favorites

Manual labor taught me the value of putting in a good day of work.

The sun was high on a late spring day. All the kids were in school, but I was home alone, out back breaking ground for a garden. I had gotten caught by one of my coaches stealing drinks out of a vending machine. Me and two other guys were running in an area outside of Baldwin High School after we broke into the coke machine. Coach Cook saw us and turned us in. Now I was clearly the best player on our team, but Coach made sure that I was held responsible for it. There was not favoritism in him because of whom I was or did my importance to the team matter. That taught me right then and there not to expect favoritism because of my athletic abilities.

So... The punishment my grandmother gave me for being expelled from school was manual labor and some time alone. I had time to think about what I had done and also miss my girl who later became my wife. (Tina) The whole ordeal was one of the life lessons that helped me form my basic beliefs, behavior and philosophy. There were a number of other small arenas and battles that had to be fought while I progressed through different levels in sports. They were all there for me to gain appreciation for the gifts given to me and to help me understand and appreciate each opportunity.

On to East Carolina University where as a team we would go from weakling trying to play against the likes of Miami Hurricanes to men actually threatening to take them out at their home venues. Coach Emory sharpened us up. The amount of talent he acquired and developed was TREMENDOUS. We battled in the weight room, at practice and in the games. Now I never had to be pushed, prodded or probed by my coaches. When practice wasn't going to well and I knew it, I took it upon myself to be the one to step it up. Sometimes coach would grab a guy and slap him on the head to wake everyone up. One day Coach Emory decided to grab me by facemask, shake me and then push kicked me. Well...I took it, looked back at him and he gave me a smile and a wink. So he said to all the other players he had no favorites but let me know what he was doing. He loved us and did whatever he could to make us better players and men.

Each of those events taught me not to expect anything to be given to me and blessed me with a humble spirit. I have had a bunch of things done because of who I am but because of my granny, Coach Cook and Coach Emory, I've never expected special treatment. Thanks for the blessing!

Notes:

_____

_____

_____

_____

• • • • • • •
Destined

Certain events in life may tend to reveal that something special is expected of you.

The player and his challenges are a constant battle of wills and the inner spirit. He grows with an undying fire for competition, while trying to be perfect and having a desire to gain victory. As he moves through the life of football or any sport, he becomes what he thinks of most. QUESTION… is there something else involved? My feel is that there is a Spirit within all actions and occurrences both on and off the field.

I can remember standing on the field in Walter B. Williams Park during what was our play-off season. I was running through the opposing team like butter, but at this moment, I was on defense standing and waiting for the opposing offense to come out of their huddle. I was standing but for some reason realized it was sleeting. For some reason I hadn't felt the cold or even realized that it was cold. I can remember that it felt like I was in a void or like a protected area. It was like I was completely alone for a while and everything just stopped. It was silent and totally peaceful.

Perhaps that was my first sense of what the zone felt like. Perhaps, the Spirit was telling me that this is one of my blessings.

There was another instance where it seemed life stood still for me. It was out in front of my mother's house in West End (Milledgeville, Ga). I was outside playing by myself. This area was where my oldest sister had laid foot to my ass a few times as well. It was a bright sunny summer day. I was running around the yard being a boy. I had a tendency to be a loner as a kid. Suddenly, I stopped and looked up at the sun. Again, I felt like everything just stopped. I looked for what seemed like hours in amazement then heard a voice tell me that I was going to coach. After that moment, I was going to school only to be a coach. I went to college and took classes for that purpose.

Right away, I started to help or let's say coach the guys that were playing with me. I started to hold them to a different standard. I became a leader and worked hard in everything I did. I can remember lifting in our weight room alone (Dangerous...had to roll 225 off my chest once). I ran each play to the fullest and wouldn't let anyone else not give their all.

I saw one of my junior high teammates at home this spring (2014). He told me about a time at practice where he was slacking off. He said I came up on him, slapped him across the head and motivated him. I don't remember doing this or other things to help, but people tell me I did. But they all reference me trying to make them better. This I feel was the coach that was being developed.

One other instance where it seemed as though time slowed to a creepy slowness was when I played at East Carolina University. We were playing William and Mary. I was handed the ball on one of our trap plays up the middle. The hole opened, so I started my acceleration but now here comes a defender from my left. He was going low and I didn't see him. He hit me directly on the outside of my left knee. Part of the blessing was I had suffered a posterior cruciate injury in the spring and was wearing a big knee
brace. My knee bent in and popped back towards the defender, and I kept on running while the defender lay down on the ground.

As life continued, my desire and natural view for coaching developed. I inspired, coached and motivated teammates along with an array of talented backs with different temperaments and talents. There were also other players that weren't in my positional influence that gravitated to me and entrusted me with their lives. The coach in me hasn't stopped coaching and the player in me hasn't stopped leading. What a blessing!

Destined? Your choice.

Notes:

_____

_____

• • • • • • •

Visualization

My first taste of visualization came from Coach Ed Emory.
It became crucial later in my career.

Visualization was a crucial part of my preparation throughout my career. Ed Emory, our head coach, introduced it to me when I attended East Carolina University. He would turn all the lights off prior to the team going out on the field and would play, "The Eye of The Tiger". Before that the locker room would be dark and silent, thus, providing some time to think and place visions in our mind. As my career advanced, I got away from the technique but would return to it from time to time.

My last three years in the NFL, I began studying on my own which lead me to watch more practice and game tape alone. When I recognized some mistakes that I had made during practice, I started to slow the tape down. To my amazement, I could see everybody's position. It allowed me to recognize when I was in a powerful or athletic position, or when I was not performing the way I desired. So while this was going on, I decided to try and visualize myself making the right step or flattening my back when I made a cut instead of having a curve in my spine. I did this while the tape was rolling in slow motion. After I got the image in my mind a couple times, I would rewind the tape back to the beginning of the play and let it flow at the regular speed, while I was visualizing the corrections that I wanted to make. It was amazing how quickly the results started to show in practice and in the games.

For everyone, there will be a different amount of time before you get the response you desire. Some will get it in days and some may take longer. But stay with it and be determined to grow.

Visualization during film and playbook study at each position is a valuable asset to today's player. With the time constraint that is stipulated by each of the governing bodies in high school and college as well as the limited time that professional players are on the field, my technique can and will help the coach and each player that practices it. This process of development can assist a player that is at any junction in his career. It can help a player that is injured recover from his injury at a faster while keeping him sharp so that when he returns to the field, it will take less time to return to his usual level of play.

The mind has been neglected for the most part in most of the athletic endeavors, although, you hear that most coaches and the people in the know say that most games are at least 80% mental. Practice these techniques for your particular position and watch your development grow as you apply them and partake in a career enhancement process. My only warning is that you have to make sure you see the play only the way you want the outcome to be. Be disciplined in your thoughts and watch the results.

Notes:

_____

_____

_____

_____

_____

_____

_____

_____

_____

_____

_____

_____

_____

_____

• • • • • • •

The Breathe

Getting into a state of equanimity was a constant battle for me. It is an area of my mind where nothing bothered me. I sought to get there whether in practice or in games.

I can remember after breaking one of the teams off with a nice run, while playing with the Redskins, R. McKenzie would come grab me and shake me like a rag doll. This happened a few times before he realized I was staying in the balance. I had made the conscious choice to neither get too high or too low. It helped me get into and stay in a zone.

The ability to get into and stay in that balanced state became a challenge for me. The trick that I was taught concerned the ability to control my breathing while focusing on what my desires were.

The ability to control the breath is a key ingredient for those trying to find and stay in the state of equanimity. Once you are able to find your rhythm the balance is available.

• • • • • • •

Use Each Experience

"He's a guy you've probably got someone like in your office. He's the kind of the guy who doesn't really want to be told. He takes it as a personal insult if you've got to say Earnest, 'You messed that up. You need to do it this way.' He'll turn around and say, 'Yah, I should have done that.' He's going to be make sure with his pride and dedication that he's going to do it right," Gibbs said.

I used mecuricome to make circles all around my Granny's house. It was fun to me. I wasn't trying to hide when I did it. It was something that came to my mind, so I did it. Well, it came to my mother's mind that I needed to be disciplined for my actions. Soooooooo, I was sent out to the switch tree to choose the branch by which I would be disciplined. Back then; we had to choose our own switch as part of the punishment. Don't come back with the small one because if she had to go out and break one off the tree....wooooweeee. Anyway, it was one of the best discipline sessions that I ever had. I remembered it for a long time. So I chose not to make any more circles in the house. I used that experience to keep the welts off my behind.

All experiences are not that dramatic, but they all need to teach us and assist us through life. I believe that we should use each experience as a tool for growth. Let's look at how I view this process in football.

Each time you are on the field, it is an opportunity to become a more complete player. The experiences that you go through can and should serve as impetuous for growth. Most players want to look at the tape of games and practice when they have a positive experience or good practice. If a guy has made a great play, he is excited about looking at the tape. Even when this is the case, the player should look at the film and observe it with thoughts of perfection. He will force himself to continue to learn.

If a player has had a difficult practice or he has had one bad play, GENERALLY, he is hesitant or anxious about watching the film and may lose sleep over the mistake. Sometimes the mind can get stuck in rewind until the next day. I would like to propose that players learn to embrace the mistakes that are made. Be willing to accept what has happened and look at it as a time for growth. Look at the play as it is, but also visualize a way that he can make the play turn out in a positive way. If this is done, the player can take the sting off the negative thoughts and in turn make them work to his advantage. While he is learning how to make the play that he missed, he also takes responsibility for the results. This can teach the player how to be responsible for his actions and also learn from all his experiences.

I really learned to watch tape this way when I was in Baltimore. I would watch the game and practice tapes alone. This technique came to me by accident. I started to do this and the next day I would get into similar situations and the correction was there. Don't be overly embarrassed about the mistake because everyone on tape will be in a similar situation, if they play long enough. Make that time a time for growth, whether positive or not.

Side note: When reviewing film, whether practice or game, it will tell a story to each player that participates. Each player has his own life within the life of the team and thus when the tape is running the tape tells only the truth about his life/performance. While watching the tape, try to get into that story as much as you can. What is the tape saying about your performance? What needs to be addressed fundamentally? What did you do well? If there is a group of guys that are a part of the team but not on the film (SUBS/PRACTICE SQUAD), they can be told a story as well. With this being the case, they should be listening and watching the story. They can hear what is said and learn from the guy on tape. If they are convinced of this and buy into the idea, the story can assist them when the time comes for them to make an appearance in their own story.

Use each experience.

Notes:

_____

_____

_____

_____

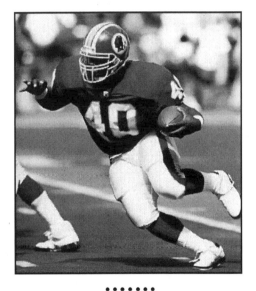

• • • • • • •

False Expectations

I wanted the opportunity to compete with Reggie Brooks and others for the job but was given an off- season demotion. My expectations lead me wrong.

They lied to me! That was the thought I had when I was brought in and given my demotion to the third down back. I won the opportunity to be "The Man", but for some reason, they could not explain that the job was being given to a young back that could not bust a grape. I was highly pissed off and disappointed in the process. I had some ideas about what I was going to achieve and work on and how I was going to take advantage of the opportunity. But they had a different vision, which made what I thought and hoped hazardous. I had some false expectations.

Have you ever had an event turn out just how you wanted it to? How excited were you when that happened? On the other hand, have you ever had a situation develop in an unexpected way? When that happens, there is a large array of emotions that show up. You may be disappointed, frustrated or even go to the extreme and become emotionally depressed. Any expectancy may have the potential to disappoint you. Whenever you go into a situation know this is a possibility. Prepare yourself for that. You may still be subject to an emotional letdown, but then you will be better equipped to deal with it and maintain your equilibrium.

Expecting something and then not obtaining the result you desire can possibly be a set up. I recommend that you maintain a balanced level of hope instead. Set your goals and go after them. Continue to be inspired by the hope of getting what you desire. By keeping hope alive, you keep yourself motivated and will in turn continue to work for what you desire. While you are working toward your goal, be sure to keep it in mind. That will keep you on target. Know why you are working and decide that you will always do your best no matter the situation.

I have one other thought. Make sure that good communication is executed between you and who you are working with or for at that time. You have to know what they expect from and out of you. If that is the case, you are insured to be working toward common goals and you can remove any question of what you should or should not be doing. When speaking with your coach or boss, make sure you are very clear. Know that he may have difficulty giving you the raw deal, so make sure you are thinking about what he might say prior to a conversation with him. Understand his position and think about some of the comments that he might have or statements that he might try to use to pacify you. Know that the BOSS is dealing with more than just you while possibly protecting the interest of the team. Make it known that you have interest in gaining understanding pertaining to you. If you can handle it, ask for complete honesty. THAT WAS IMPORTANT FOR ME!

Notes:

_____

_____

_____

• • • • • • •

Work with a Purpose

I had Chris Johnson look at me during this drill.
The purpose was to reinforce his feel.

Along with visualization, a positive affirmation will make your workouts more productive and give you better results. Each athlete should always do drills in a way that will carry over into their respective sports. Do the drill in the position your body will be in while playing the sport. In each drill, you should be able to see why you are performing the task, make the drill fit your sport, and it will assist you in becoming more productive. If a drill or exercise is not helping you, then you must find a way to tweak it and make it applicable. This takes me to the concept of practicing well.

When practicing, no matter the speed of the drills, get your body into the proper position to perform the task. Do all repetitions the way you would perform them in a game. When you do this, you will not waste valuable time and energy doing a task improperly. When an athlete performs a drill improperly, they are not just being lazy. They are conditioning themselves to perform the task incorrectly. It takes a lot of discipline to do this, but if you truly want to be successful, you will definitely find that the energy is worth it.

When in practice, make sure that each time you run a play you perform that assignment like you are reacting in a game. So many times I see players start a play with the right mentality and decided that they have done enough before the whistle is blown. I'm sure you have heard the old saying, "you play like you practice." It's absolutely true. If you perform a task well in practice, it carries over to the game and the flip side is also applicable. If you perform the task poorly over time, it will end up hurting you when you least expect it. I have seen many receivers catch the ball and run past defenders like they will not be hit. That might be the case in practice, but in the game you have to defend yourself. So, while you are in practice you might as well get used to dropping your weight and get into those positions that will be required in a game. The same goes for all positions. Prepare yourself the best way you can on every play. React and be proactive. Be the way you would want it in the game.

Notes:

_____

_____

_____

_____

_____

•••••••
Solutions...Problems

Always return to your basics.

Always work for yourself. Focus on improvements and desires. If something or some part of your game needs to be improved, work at it, focus on it, and keep it in mind. It is not what others think you need to do, but instead, it is what you think you need to do that is important. I'm not saying don't listen to your coaches. I always felt like true development comes from within. If you have true self-awareness, then you know yourself best. Yes, you will and should learn from others. It's a way of growth as well. If you are honest with yourself, then you can be your best coach.

Talk to your coach, be very observant and be a critic of your own performance. Pick something out and start working on this area as you watch film. Remember, you can start by visualizing the change that you want to make. Next write it down, so you can confirm and reaffirm it. When practice begins and the individual drills are practiced, use this time to start working on one thing that you want to improve.

If you are focused, then you can grow at a methodical and consistent rate. If you are trying to improve your game without real direction then it's like throwing a bunch of "stuff" at the wall seeing what will stick. Build your mansion by starting with and returning to your basics. They are your foundation. Anytime you struggle or have success, go back to your basics. It will keep you grounded.

Each year I would return home (Milledgeville, GA) to run hills. I would run intervals on my old HS track. To me, this was a way of going back home to my base and foundation.

Notes:

_____

_____

_____

_____

_____

• • • • • • •
Overcoming Obstacles

Always seek to grow. Perfection is sought...progress accepted....

MENTAL strength and courage are needed to produce under fire. Game time conditions can bring out the doubts and fears that an athlete has. The weaknesses in an individual's personality have a way of manifesting themselves on the field. As you know, we look for perfection whether we are in our professional or personal lives. We should ascribe to be perfect, but know that we will fall short. Now, part of the deal should be that we have no self-debasement when the imperfection shows up. Better yet, the determinate as far as the individual's happiness is concerned is how well we handle setbacks. Do we become distraught, cry, get down on ourselves, or become angry? I must say, there are places for all of these emotions if we can learn to understand what the root cause is. We can seek understanding or gain knowledge while asking questions about the purpose that this is serving in our life. Ask yourself what can I learn from this situation?

It's been my experience that after all the emotions have subsided, that's when the life lesson appeared right before my eyes. When I reflect on the situation, it has always been there. So the question is, do we learn to accept less or try to become excellent in our chosen field? I would suggest that we always look for the betterment of any skill. The result will be a continuous push for excellence and an incessant desire that continues to motivate us daily. This desire can turn into an obsession or a driving tool if used properly. I actually came within one play of having a perfect game in the 1987 play-offs vs. the Indianapolis Colts. On that particular day my pass protection, running the rock, and pass catching out of the backfield were on point. I was in the zone. The zone was on, but I had to have that one play that gave me some additional motivation. Even if I had played the perfect game, there would have been something that I still needed to improve on.

So what am I saying to you? Simply what is seen as an obstacle is only the next challenge. Each experience should serve as an opportunity for you to grow. The only thing that can get in the way of your progress is you and your understanding.

Side note: Reflection is a powerful tool that can be used in all facets of life. If you have had an event during the day that you would like to improve on, spend some time thinking about the situation and think through ways that you can or could have made the event turn out differently. Quiet time is crucial in the process. Spend time alone with no distractions and let your mind focus on what you truly desire. If this is difficult for you initially, start out with short moments and then extend the time as you become more comfortable.

Just know that with reflection something special is within your grasp.

Notes:

_____

_____

_____

_____

_____

_____

_____

• • • • • • •
Media Battles

Take nothing personal regarding the media. It's a job.

I once played/worked for a coach that took what was said by the media extremely personally. He spent a lot of time worrying about his image and what was said. HIs thought process was they are out to get me. He spent too much time worrying about what he couldn't control.

There is a saying that "you should believe none of what you hear and half of what you see." With that being said, we have to take whatever is in the press, whether printed or spoken, as someone just doing his or her job. The main purpose of the media is to sell whatever product they represent. There will be some give and take. Know that you will be a hero one day and the next they can't wait to bring you to your knees. If you have an issue with something written or said about you, then talk to the individual about it. Do this after you have had time to cool off and have thought about whether what was said happened to be true or not. Be honest with yourself first and foremost then look at the situation objectively. Make sure it's just you two and no emotions involved.

Making an issue with something that is said or done by someone in the media will serve as a battleground that you don't want to be a part of and a battle that you can't win. You may be able to tell a reporter off, but in the end they have the last word. You might be able to get something off your chest. What purpose does an argument serve? It may give your opponent a motivation.

Frustrations will come one day. When they do, they should be dealt with as quickly as possible so everyone involved can move on and be cleansed of the negative energy associated. When frustration is within, don't allow it to remain within the body of the individual or of the team.

If there is an issue with the coach or organization pertaining to the media and how you have been represented, then deal with it in house. Fighting battles about what the coach, organization or someone else on the team has said is one way to tear down the team's integrity. It can get someone pushed out of the door. This again is a no-win situation, so bite your tongue and focus on what you have to do to get your job done. What people think of you should be based on your actions. Let your play and how you do your job speak for you. Don't let your pride be your downfall.

· · · · · · ·
Job's on the Line

Whether practicing or playing, jobs are always on the line.

At the end of the 1993 season, Joe Gibbs decided to retire. I was on my way back from the grocery store when the news flash hit the airwaves. The dread said to me that my career just hit another path. I was very uncertain about where I would be playing football the next year or whether I would be doing it at all. My job and life was on the line.

Petibone ended up being named the head coach. I was demoted to third down back before we got to off-season training. No competition to make sure that the position improved or the team better.

Have you ever been concerned that you would not have a job at the end of a fiscal year? Has this disconcerting feeling ever gripped you in such a way that it affected your sleep patterns and family life? These concerns affect some of the players at the end of each season.

A guy that is on the lower tier of the team, a guy that has aged, or has had to deal with a season ending injury may have to consider that their lives will change. They may have to look beyond where their careers have been for a majority of their lives and search for a new beginning. The new beginning might be with another team or it might be a totally new arena where they may have to become a rookie all over again. This energy can be crippling and can even spring up while the season is going on.

Let's say that a guy has not dressed for a game because he is on the inactive list. What is his future? If he is a young guy, maybe he is being developed and just biding some time. But if he is an older player that can't crack the 53-man roster, he might be recognizing the signs that his career is coming to an end.

The league that I work in and the one you know are full of constant transitions. These transitions are fueled by the salary cap and the need to find good, quality players, but for cheaper deals. It truly is a young man's game. This means that there are a lot of jobs that could go to older more stable athletes that are for sale. In my opinion, the league itself is getting younger and the parity will keep rising. Did I say jobs for sale?

So, how do you handle a situation like this? How can you produce under this type of pressure and try to ensure that you have a better opportunity the following year? Again, the best thing is for each player to focus on the things that he can control. His attitude towards the job and the work environment are crucial while he recognizes the bigger. If he can do this, then he can produce.

So yeah, the job is on the line all the time and if the player and coach are wise, they will go about each day with that awareness in the back of their mind. Focus on doing your best each day and for that matter each moment.

Now that you are armed with a bit of understanding and given a perspective, keep an eye open for these types of happenings around the league. When one of your favorite players just disappears on you, the salary cap or an injury may have played a part. It's a sad thing, but it is true.

Notes:

_____

_____

_____

_____

_____

_____

_____

_____

_____

_____

_____

•••••••
Define and Redefine

Change is constant! Rest when you are sleep.

Constant defining and redefining while keeping your foundation in tact is a must and is a main stay for Super Bowl Champs and winners. That is what looking for perfection looks like. We aim to be the best we can be while understanding that perfection is an illusion.

The choice to keep pushing myself to get better each day was and is a gift from the Spirit. While as a player this gave me ideas to make me a better player while also prepared me to become a good coach.

The same mentality and energy that was a gift to me from the Spirit allowed me to continue to assist the backfield participants. They were the expression of what foundation we laid as well as continued to fine tune. Being able to get them ready to perform at a high level with the additions I was given has prepared me for what's next.

I've come to a phase that might take me in a multitude of directions, but rest assured that I have been prepared. For I continued to redefine how I coached and the gifts that the Spirit birthed while I coached the starter in my rooms all the way down to the guy that was on the practice squad, has brought me to this place.

Love of each experience whether good, bad or indifferent, provides the energy to move to the next phase.

Be blessed.

Notes:

_____

_____

_____

_____

_____

_____

_____

_____

. . . .
Energy Transfer

The ability to use positive or negative emotions, anger or excitement to achieve your desires.

The ability to take the experience and use it, whether positive or negative, is an ability we all have. Pain, illness and all range of emotions can be a source of energy to get done what is required. Choosing to take that energy on to the next experience is a constant decision.

At Baldwin High School, in Milledgeville, Georgia, while practicing, I dropped a ball that was normally an easy catch. As a guy that takes the game to heart on all occasions, this provoked in me anger. When I got in the huddle my mind was clear, but there was something that felt different to me about the next play. I seemed to be more aware of what I needed to do.

The next play I was handed the ball and was confronted by one of our defenders. I made him miss and then broke the next tackle to go on and finish 30 yards down the field.

Instead of me languishing in the mistake, which is easily done, I went on to the play with the feeling of doing something to make amends. My teammates and I benefited.

I can remember playing the Colts on a Monday night game. Eric Dickerson was the back for them, so that within itself was enough motivation to play at a high level. That motivation was one of the ways that pushed me to play at a high level.

During the game, I had an AC joint separation. Now you know I was not leaving the game even though I was in pain. Art Monk and Gary Clark kept telling me to go to the sideline. I kept refusing.

I was able to settle the pain down in between plays and focus it so I could go on to make the plays that helped keep us in the game. We did not win, but I was able to take the pain and transfer it into the energy needed to play.

Energy transfer can be used when you notice one side of the body is weaker than the other in doing the same task. If you recognize that weakness then you can transfer the feeling that you have in the stronger side to the weaker. For example if you have a significant injury to your right ankle and you are trying to rehab, perform a task (let's say toe raises) with your left. Feel it then do it right away with you right while thinking of the left. This thought process can actually help with the strengthening process and may even help with healing.

Use your energy to transfer into whatever you desire. The mind is a beautiful thing.

Notes:

_____

_____

_____

_____

_____

_____

_____

_____

• • • • • • •

Temper Temper

Weaknesses can also be our strengths.

Is it true that when someone gets mad or lose their temper they also temporally lose their sanity? I do feel that is a truism. With that base as my premise, I was insane quite a few times while growing up.

I was known as a hot head. Fighting was my quick reaction when someone did something I felt was unjust no matter if it was done to me or someone I knew. Those fights were in life, but even more when I was on the football field.

I would fight my teammates while at practice if I felt they weren't giving their all. If a defender did something against the rules... FIGHT! That temper was the part of the fuel that helped me develop as a player. It drove me to also drive others close to me. But what's a gift can also be a curse.

While reflecting on my life, I saw early in my life that I despised losing. My temper was evident even as a young kid while playing marbles. We played marbles as neighborhood kids. I was decent at it and enjoyed playing. We would play a game called keepers. We would draw a circle in the sand then place some of each guy's marbles inside. We would take turns shooting to knock the opponents marbles out of the circle. When you knocked them out you could keep them and as long as you were in the circle you kept shooting. Carl Cummings was good and would get on a roll. He won a lot, but I would force him to give me my marbles back. Carl never stopped playing with me. We remained friends all the way through school. Thanks for accepting me Carl.

My temper would flare up in games as well. Again this was a way of intimidating some of our opponents, so it served to be an advantage because if I as a leader didn't take any sh__ (stuff), then it set the stage. Well we were playing the bad ass Oilers in the 1988 playoffs at home. We hated them and they hated us. So... we are driving the ball late in the game and one of their defenders got in my face after a play and I reacted. A high percentage of the time when I acted it was ok. This time it cost us 15 yards. Damn... well that's not all; I kept going for some reason! Another 15 yards. Damn, we are out of field goal range. We lose to an inferior team because, in part, of my temper. A curse!

Learning through that experience took me years. Having temporary insanity can't be an excuse for costing the team. My awareness was raised because of it. It allowed me to play with a tremendous edge and brutality, but I had to learn to harness it and redirect it, so the benefit could be attained.

Notes:

_____

_____

_____

_____

_____

_____

_____

_____

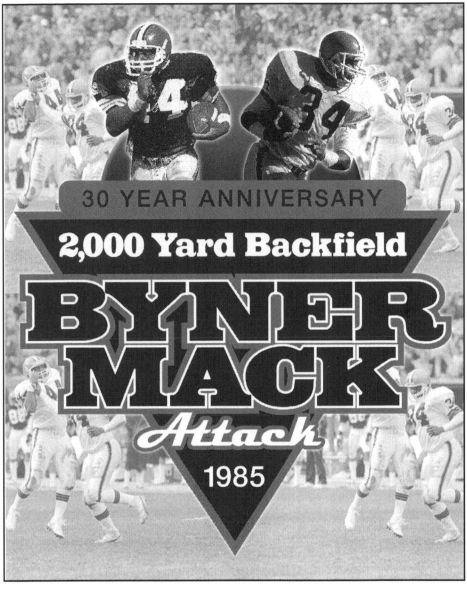

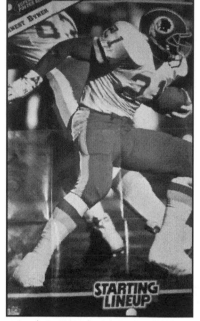

TOTAL YARDAGE	Rush	Rec	Total
E. BYNER	432	552	984
K. MACK	735	223	958

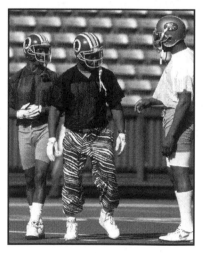

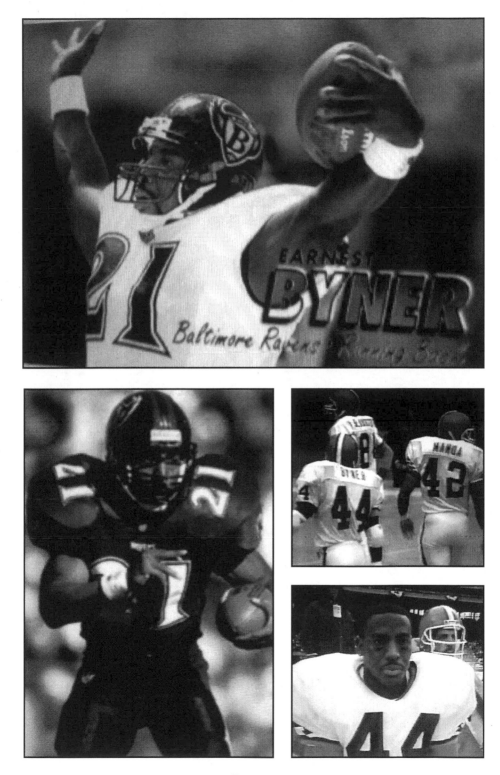

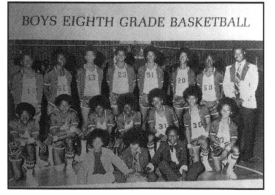

Football Philosophy

•••••••
For the Love of the Game

I was extremely HOT when Al Lavan told me they were going to start Bam Morris over me. The picture shows me on the sideline with him and Marchibroda.

I burst out the back door excited about the possibility of going to the park to play two-hand touch football with the neighborhood kids. I got all my chores done with my granny, so I could get to the field. We loved to play against each other and the other neighborhoods. It was a way to bond and keep us out of trouble. We played because we loved it and enjoyed the competition that it provided. It was our first impression of the sport and the main reason we played. The love of the game kept us thrilled and excited. Initially, I played for the fun of the game. Why else does anyone begin to play any sport? It gave me a level of assurance of who I was and what I can make happen while enjoying the thrill of victory. It brings about a sense of belonging while bringing out the best and exposing the worst. First and foremost is the plain old love and enjoyment of trying to go beyond your wildest dreams, to find victory when defeat seems imminent. When this thrill hits you, you know it. It can't be replaced by anything else.

There are many reasons to play the game. Wanting to be famous, rich, or a legend are three possible reasons. Any of those may be the reason to play, but rarely will anyone start out with this in mind.

The ecstasy of victory is real. The energy associated with winning doesn't last, but we love it when we do win. You have an athletic arrogance. You know and he knows that you are better. What a grand feeling.

Don't ever forget this thrill and why you truly play the game. It is easy to get caught up in the "why me" syndrome. Why did they do this to me? Why won't they treat me fairly? I don't know why they treat him better than me. Don't fall for it. Remember why you started to play the game.

When you start seeing the politics game it may cause you to lose desire and the initial love you have. This is a trick that can steal your heart away and cause lost opportunities when they arise. An opportunity can be lost because of the negative feelings that have kept you from preparing and staying focused on what you can control. The control that you have can only be exercised on yourself and not on the others that you think may be making the decisions that are keeping you from reaching your goals. This can be a vicious cycle as you can see. So I must say, focus on you and what can be done to make your dreams come true. Stay away from the tape that can run and re-run in your head. This tape will have you focused on things you can't control while not allowing you to focus on what you can. This tape can be called the "if only". If only this or if only that I would do... The best way to work this is to just plain old keep it simple.

In 1997, while I was in Baltimore, the team decided to start Bam Morris over me. He was younger, bigger, and stronger but he had been suspended for the first four games of the season. Another player was supposed to start, but I had beaten him out. Experience over youth, you know. I was named the starter and we began the season on a decent run. I played well, but could have done some things better. I always look at what I can change to make things come out differently. When it was time for Bam to come back, there was no reason to destroy the chemistry on offense. At the time, we were moving the ball and scoring points. But they decided to move me anyway. Al Lavan broke the news to me. I started crying right there in the meeting. It hurt, really hurt me bad, and the explanation was no good. He told me it was nothing I had done, but they were going to make the move. You were talking about not helping someone with a key transition. I'll be damned!!

After serving 10 years in the league and having gone through a similar situation in Washington, I went on to look at myself and ask the hard questions concerning my contribution to the situation. Earlier in my career I would have been more disappointed and a lot more upset. This happened to me when the Redskins decided to replace me with Reggie

Brooks after Joe Gibbs had retired and Richie Pettibon became the head coach. They didn't even give me a chance to fight for the job. They just made the decision in the off-season because they knew if they made it a fair fight, then I would stand a good chance to win it. I fussed and fought about it for a while. I got extremely pissed off and a few times walked away from practice, throwing my helmet on the ground because there was no way this guy was better than I was. I knew it and...well, enough said.

Hey, you want more info, huh?

Even in this case I eventually decided to do something about the situation instead of staying with that negative energy. After a pre-season game, I decided that I was going to improve my conditioning instead of just not doing anything. The next day, Alvoid Mays and I went to George Mason and ran some hills even though it was supposed to be our day off. Side note: I believe this was the impetus for me to extend my career another four years. First, having a friend and second, going to the hill for some self-improvement. So don't focus on the situation you are in. Rather, focus on how you contributed to the situation and what you can do to prepare for what life has to offer you in the future. The relationships that you have with the guys and the teammates of yesteryear are all reasons to play. These are relationships that you will be able to take with you when it is time for you to leave the game. If you enjoy every day, then you will be focused on the positives and not on the "what if" that can hinder your process.

The other thing I did came to me very naturally due to the coach in me. I went on to help Reggie Brooks and Bam Morris prepare for the games and did everything in my power to help my teammates be the best they could be and therefore help the team win. That also helped take away the negative energy. Focusing on someone other than yourself is a tremendous way you can get over disappointment and keep your mind on why you really got involved in the game.

Focus on why you play the game, the love of it and the feeling that it brings when victory is gained.

Notes:

_____

_____

• • • • • • •

True Development

Always push yourself to continue developing your talents. Continue looking inside to find your vision.

We had just won the Super Bowl and we were back at the hotel. It was 1992. We were in Minnesota and had defeated the Bills 35-24 to become Super Bowl XXVI champs. Instead of basking in the glow of just winning the big one, my thoughts were of what we would do next. I felt the need to go to the next game and to keep moving forward. There was one problem. There was not another game. I still wasn't satisfied because I felt like I could play better. The taste for me could not be satisfied.

Becoming the player you desire to be takes commitment, luck, and constant evaluation of the progress that you have made and the improvement you desire. A very strong and positive way to grow is reflection. Thinking back on your performance and the way that the events unfolded can help you decide how you will respond or be proactive the next time you confront a similar situation. When you study film from your practice or game, what is it that you are doing? Reflecting. Reflecting is a way in which you can watch what you have done, notice that outcome, and make adjustments if needed. One key to this is to make sure that you are as picky as possible. We have a tendency to be easily pleased and become complacent with a positive result. If you are to last a long time and continue to mature, there must be a desire every day to get better.

If what you say about being the best does not match up with the actions you produce then you must question your true desire and commitment. If you say you want to be the best and you fall asleep in the meeting, you need to reconsider your statement. Instead, you might say you are happy just where you are. I say that if you want to be the best, but you stay out late drinking heavily, you might need to rethink what your true desire is.

Point being is that you should make sure that you want to be committed to excellence. Even though perfection is an illusion, it should not keep you from pursuing the perfect game.

Make sure you have fun doing what you desire to do. Relax, have a drink or two, smoke a cigar, or do whatever you desire. But make sure it is not to the detriment of your success. When it's time to rest and relax, take the time to get away. This will help you to rejuvenate so when it's time to work, you can go at it with all you have. So, when you get the opportunity to get away make sure that you take full advantage of it.

Notes:

_____

_____

_____

_____

_____

_____

_____

_____

• • • • • • •

One Mentality of the Athlete

Getting an understanding of the athletic mind.

We start out playing the game that we love because we love it. As time moves on, development becomes an intricate part of the athlete's mentality. That old saying is that either you get better or you get better. Actually, that's my saying.

I feel like on each day and in each situation there is room for development. If you take the opportunity to learn from the experience, then you make progress. So, either you get better or you really get better. As development continues and if the athlete is proud the effects of the development, then it starts to become part of the individual. He may start to take success or non-success personally.

As an athlete progresses along the natural path of maturation, the scrutiny that he is placed under intensifies. The level of coverage a mistake is given can be mind blowing. Because of the level of support that is given to sports in our country, our players and their actions are seen as even more important. Both on and off the field behaviors are big news. The coverage of the team and the need to have someone blamed for a loss or be made a hero, drives how the stories are written and perceived. As we all know, the negative gets the most attention in the mind of the fan and the athlete. Bad publicity is still publicity.

The positive and the negative can be looked upon as an extension of the athlete. When I state that the athlete lives his success or non-success very personally, I am really speaking about the non-successes because those are the ones that stand out the most. The negative stings stick and stay. When it's at the level of major college or professional sports, it becomes even more intense. When I fumbled the ball in Denver, I felt like I let everyone down on my team and in my family. That hurt me so deeply! I can't even explain to you what it did to me. Yes, I stood up and faced the media and told them that I left everything out on the field, which was true. But I was struggling and did not know how the media would handle it.

I was the next day's news all over the country, perhaps the world, and I was the next week talk show joke. I even had people tell me about some of the jokes that were said in their way of informing me while trying to make light of the situation. Now, initially I was okay and knew that the play was in the flow of the game. But everyone else wanted it to be a constant part of my thought process. The travesty was that I let it stay with me based on what others thought instead of how my true friends and I thought. I did not deal with that situation properly, so it stayed with me and affected me while I was away from football and as I continued to play. It stayed on my mind so much that while playing the next couple years, I would go down on the play to make sure I didn't fumble the ball instead of fighting for yards like I did prior to the Denver game. It took me about three years before I finally forgave myself and moved on.

My point is that this is a way an athlete can be looked upon and how he may possibly be affected by the exposure of his mistakes. In knowing that the media has a job to do they must consider that the players are learning and growing in each experience and are trying to move past their mistakes on a continual path of development.

I can remember racing against Buddy Colt when I was in the 6th, 7th, and 8th grades. He would always beat me. Now I was one of the faster guys everywhere I went. But this guy had me. My confidence was always down when I knew I had to race him until I decided to focus on me instead of him. I beat him!! Woooooweee! I felt invincible and felt like I could beat anyone I raced against thereafter. The success that I had against Buddy propelled me forward full of confidence. The mounting successes that an athlete has and the effect it can have on the mind can produce huge growth in confidence. Confidence is built to a supreme high because with each success there is growth in the belief that he can get the job done. Personal momentum is what I would like to call it. It's a time when you feel like you can do anything you desire. It carries over into all facets of your life. The air about you is different. The people you run into can sense it. Some people think an athlete is stuck up at this time or he thinks his stuff doesn't stink. For the most part it's not about that, but some people do get the big head. This is when they should watch out because life's balance is on its way.

The balance happened to me in Denver. The game before that one we played Indy at home. I had a tremendous day. It was a retribution game for me because I had fumbled the ball against Indy during the regular season at a critical part of the game. I had a day that was almost perfect. I was one play away from the perfect game. I had a tendency to get better and stronger as the year went on. I was in that mode again. So when we got ready to play Denver in the Championship game, I had the air I spoke about. During the warm up process I felt great. One of the reporters covering the game said to me, "Have a good game", as we were heading back to the locker room. I told him "I WILL"! It wasn't that I just said this. It was I felt and believed it without a doubt. I had a great game but my feeling of invincibility was balanced out.

Life has a way of balancing all of its experiences. With each negative experience there will be a positive one as well. If an athlete understands this then he should prepare as if the next experience can be that balance and take him from goat to hero. If he can look at the mistake and be motivated to try harder and prepare more diligently then he will be ahead of the curve and continue on towards what he truly desires.

Mistakes will be made and focused on. We all know everyone makes them (Everybody Fumbles), but the true champions look at each mistake as a new challenge. If used correctly, they will propel them forward.

Notes:

_____

_____

_____

_____

_____

_____

_____

_____

• • • • • • •
Finish Each Play

There are play clocks that sometime dictate the outcome of plays. The whistle should be your clock.

One play that really stands out happened when I played for the Cleveland Browns. We were playing the Colts during the 86/87 football year. We had played a good game, but they were ahead late in the game. We mounted a comeback and were driving for a possible tying field goal and perhaps a winning TD. I was handed the ball on a simple gut play to the left. They had the play stopped, and I knew I was going to be tackled. I relaxed before I got to the ground and the ball came out. They recovered and won the game. I RELAXED!

Relaxing can happen when a lineman, backfield participant or tight end is pass blocking and they feel like the QB should have thrown the ball. They relax and the defender keeps rushing and gets a sack. The announcers may say it was a hustle sack. It may very well seem that way, but the blocker knows he let up to early.

Earnest Byner's *Everybody Fumbles*

At times there is a tendency to play until you think the play should be over. There have been many plays that were and will be made because someone decided before the play was over that the play was over. Finish the play and play until the whistle has blown, so you won't be the victim of the "if syndrome". We have all been there at one time or another, so make sure you learn from it and make a decision that it won't happen again.

Learn from my experience. Never relax. A better saying is ALWAYS PLAY TO THE WHISTLE. FINISH!

Notes:

_____

_____

_____

_____

_____

_____

_____

_____

_____

_____

_____

_____

_____

_____

•••••••
Thinking Game

Art Monk was one of the most unselfish players. He was a man who understood how to think and play the game.

Ark Monk had been with the Redskins for seven or eight years by the time I was traded to Washington from Cleveland. I sat near him when we were in the big room as Joe Gibbs was covering the installation of the offense. I observed him taking notes every day that we were in the classroom. He did this even though he had been in the offense the entire time that Joe was the head coach. He could have easily convinced himself that he has it down because it's what he had done year after year. He chose to continue to learn and relearn. I believe he did this so that when the plays were called, the assignments would be innate and his play was not hindered because of thinking.

Cerebral players are the players that can think of all the little things that go with each play when the play is called. They can turn off the thinking portion of the game when the ball is snapped. How does this happen? The playbook has become innate for this player. The player has spent some time in his playbook while at home, and this player has decided to take notes while in the classroom. He is motivated by the thought of playing the perfect game. So he is a detail-oriented guy. When the play is called in the huddle, he goes through the reminders along with the adjustment that might have to be made. As he lines up and takes a look at the opponent, he has a plan of action while thinking of the assignment. Now, when the ball is snapped its time to forget all the thinking and just play the game. Let the natural abilities take over and let the inner eye guide you as the play proceeds.

Now, experience will teach you how to think as you play and assist you in being aware of the down, distance, and the conditions of the game. With that knowledge you will be able to make adjustments as you play. Ask yourself questions like, do I need to get out of bounds or stay in and get additional yards? Each situation requires a level of planned action while still being able to play the game.

When I was at the Redskins as a coach, I had a prominent player tell me he had to think too much. I taught him that no matter what level you play; using your brainpower is a requirement. In the test, interviews and background checks that are done, one of the main points of interest by anyone choosing players is thinking ability.

So, be a thinker and be mentally disciplined when the game is happening. If you can stay disciplined while practicing, then you have the ability to be focused in the game. It's a matter of making the choice to concentrate during the preparation stage and to be clear and focused at practice.

Side note for game day: While the game is going on there will be coaching points that can and will be given to you about what is thought to be happening on the field. The information for the most part is good, so the player needs to listen and take heed, but also know what is happening for himself. Make sure that you are always in a position of learning. Most good coaches will ask you, what did you see? They will do this before making comments about what they think or before giving any suggestions. That is why you have to know the game plan and know what you have seen on the field. When asked about what is happening and what has happened, be as clear as possible and be honest. Don't try to lie about something if you don't know. If you make a mistake, say it and be ready to move on. Keep your mind in the game even if the coach seems to give too much info or second-guesses you. It's not a personal attack. It is the way he thinks the job must be done. So stay focused. Know what you need to do. Players play on game day. Coaches do most of the teaching during the week.

Notes:

_____

_____

_____

_____

_____

·······

Confidence

"Coach (EB) showed me a couple runs from Denver when I made the second level and made people miss and he said, 'We need to get this guy back,'" Portis said. "It's been awhile since I got to the second level, competing against safeties, punishing people, making people miss."

For any athlete to be successful there has to be a level of talent, confidence, and a good mind. It has been said that success builds confidence. Confidence is something that can be achieved through various resources. One resource that I have used is old material or game footage of the players or myself.

A player might be going through a difficult time and probably has been taking a beating in the area of confidence. When one of my guys can't seem to fight his way out of the funk and I recognize it, I go to the film department and ask one of the guys to make a tape of the player with only his good plays. I watch the tape with the player and point out the positives. While watching it, I instruct him to feel the energy it took to make the plays on the tape. I also ask him to put himself back in the game so he can tap into that, then he can start to bring himself out of the funk. As he watches the film/videotape, he can then see what plays were successful for him in the past. The talk with him before the tape is turned on starts with him thinking and then the tape reaffirms what has been initiated by the conversation. Once I have gone through the process with him, I have the player watch it in his own.

Another player that needs confidence is a player returning from an injury that has caused him to miss a substantial amount of time. The tape of previous success can be ideal for this player along with visualization. I recommend using the thoughts of games even when the player can't be active. Give him purpose instead of just the drudgery of rehab.

Another player who might need this is a player that has been benched. Obviously, confidence has taken a beating here, but you can also deal with someone who has lost a level of desire to play. So getting out the old tape can be just what the doctor ordered.

To assist the player further, he should be reminded of his purpose in the game. Why does he put himself through the process of off-season training and why does he try to do what is right? The purpose should be as simple as wanting to be the very best that he can be. Every day there should be some type of challenge. Think about it, feel it and place it in the mind's eye.

Some players get caught up in 'what are they going to do to me today?' They are the coaches, scouts, GMs and of course anyone other than the player. Guys with that mentality are always looking outside for answers instead of asking the one question needed. What did I do to allow this to happen? Being able to ask that is critical to his growth.

The process of worrying about the things that cannot be controlled will wear the individual down and slowly take away confidence. Just do the best that you can everyday and in every way that you can. When you know that you have deposited all that you can in the bank of your career, then you can be satisfied with that. What may come to you might not be what you want, but one thing is for sure, it will be what you need at that time. Trust yourself first and foremost, then look outside to gain more strength and confidence in what the inner spirit is providing.

Notes:

_____

_____

_____

_____

_____

_____

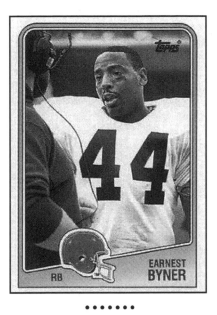

• • • • • • •

Leadership

Speaking with the "Mad Scientist" Howard Mudd on the sideline.

A true leader will recognize the responsibility and the power he has on the team. With this recognition, there are actions taken because of their responsibilities that accompany the leadership role.

Many people have told me how I affected the team when I was with the Cleveland Browns. My former coach, Howard Mudd, shared memories with me. He recalled to me the practices before a playoff game vs. the Miami Dolphins in 1985. On the Thursday prior to the game, the coaching staff kept me out of the inside run period. Coach Mudd told me that I was so intense. He told me that I would not allow anyone to be unprepared or let anyone settle for less than their best. I must admit that I was crazy at times. They called me, "The Tasmanian Devil."

I tell you this with total honestly. I do not remember most of what I did. I was doing what was natural to me. I lived the moment to the fullest and did what was called for in each situation. I loved each one of my teammates and wanted what was best for them. It is just as I love my players now and want the best for them, both on and off the field.

A leader speaks strongly about what actions that need to be taken and what type of conduct and effort is expected, but he must also model these same behaviors as best he can. Remember no one is perfect, but we seek to be. Purity of his motives must be clear to all that are under his control and influence.

A leader can influence the entire team and can drive them to higher expectations and therefore, a higher degree of success. Some lead on higher levels than others, but the leadership within the player ranks should be recognized and focused on. It's needed.

A leader must be able to communicate with the Head Coach in a way that shows respect, and in doing so, he raises the level of respect that the coach has for him. There should always be a protocol within the team, which should always be respected and honored. It's about being a doer, and not merely just a talker, even when you don't feel like it. It not only requires a demand from yourself, but also a demand from others. It's a willingness to sacrifice for the betterment of all of the teammates involved. This sacrifice may involve taking the blame for a loss when it is clearly not your fault. This sacrifice may involve standing for the team and standing up for what is right.

This person should not have selfish motives when he is supposed to speak for the team. Even if his motives appear selfish, they need to serve for the overall betterment of the team.

When you have leaders that are like this, then you have people who will be mentors to your younger players. You know what type of locker room you will have. If you don't have these types of leaders, then you will have to watch for possibilities and begin the training process.

I am constantly asking this from our guys on both sides of the ball to take hold of this position of influence. I have a room full of potentials that I coach. Chris Johnson (Tennessee Titans) and Ahmard Hall (Tennessee Titans) were two players that I recently coached who had this potential. They are dynamic individuals, all looking to be the best and their play has put them in a position to lead. However, they do not always welcome it, as it is not comfortable for some players. If the team wants to become champions, players who step into a role have to step up. Sometimes, to get them there the push is gentle. Other times, the push has to be more forceful.

Winning championships requires leadership within the player ranks. Do not be afraid of the influence you have young men. Be the one that is the difference, so that one day they are saying it was because of you that we became winners.

Notes:

• • • • • • •
Leadership Part 2

Positive influence is needed in your locker rooms.
Working to develop that is a challenge

I mentioned that Chris Johnson (Tennessee Titans) and Ahmard Hall (Tennessee Titans) were driven and wanted to be the best. In no way was I suggesting that that they needed a push. They are good men of the game in all ways, but as with all players, they need and deserve coaching.

In all of the rooms that I have been in charge of and in those that I have assisted in, leadership from each position was and will continue to be one of the main ingredients for a team's success. Jim Brown said, "The running back position is the premier position in football." I believe that this still holds true today. The running back position shouts out leadership.

We all know that whomever is at the top of an organization is the leader of organization. He or she is the tone-setter for the entire team or organization. The buck stops there. We also know that the people hired by the organization have to take the leader's message and share it with players that they are responsible for.

With that said, on a football team there are certain areas that are considered sacred. One place is the locker room. I have walked into a bunch of them as a player, coach, and administrator. I can tell you that as one of the latter two, when I do walk in, the players sometimes make this siren sound. Some of it is in jest, but some of it is distrust. I felt both of those as a player as well, but I know that we are all ultimately working for the same reasons. Winning! I will always be comfortable in there because it's my background, but I know it is considered holy ground.

What are you saying EB? I am telling you that players have more influence over other players than you can imagine. That is why if you have a bad seed in the locker room and if things are not going well, the bad seed can end up killing the team. On another level, if you have good leaders, and if things in the locker room start to go wrong, then the leaders will be there to help keep the locker room focused on the winning ways.

If you watch some highlight tapes or listen to stories that are told, you hear about times where things could have gone in a completely different direction, but someone stood in the gap. This, my friend, is an example of someone being the leader within the locker room.

As I have said before, good leadership can be a team saver.

Here we go baby!

Notes:

_____

_____

_____

_____

_____

_____

_____

_____

_____

• • • • • • •
Getting Ready

Another aspect of visualization and mental development.

Fear and anxiety started to get into me when I was in Washington. The year was 1990 and it felt like I might be losing something. A young linebacker was practicing the way he needed to get ready to play, but he was knocking me around while he was doing it. I decided to look at the defense and visualize the team that we were going to play Sunday. The feelings of fear and anxiety I had, dissipated and I worked on the same foot, same shoulder drill to defeat the young backer at the same time. (Thanks Joe Pendry),

When each player is getting ready for the game in practice sessions, employ him or her to visualize the colors of the opponent they will play that week. It will make the practice mean more to them and can give the player additional energy to get through the practices during the week.

There will be some that might say that this will make some players peak early, but the reality of the situation is that when the lights come one and the ball is kicked off, an additional surge of energy is supplied due to live action. The fans and the TV cameras all add to the energy that is brought on game day.

With this method of visualization, the player can practice and be prepared to perform and play the game at a higher level. One additional way to improve the visualization technique is in film study or practice. Each player can again visualize how he wants the play to be performed or how he wants to use a specific technique to perform a specific task. Watch the tape as it is and take notes of what you did. Then look at the tape the way you want the play to be executed. If you can visualize the play the way you want it to be, then you can start making the adjustments necessary while you are in the meeting room. Watching the tape in slow motion will assist the player in recognizing when the body is in a strong position or when it is in a weak position. After this recognition, the player can visualize or make the adjustment in a step-by-step manner. If the player has the ability or will to take the time, with or without the coach (preferably with), he can run the tape in slow motion. This will allow him and the coach the ability to see the flaws that can't be seen at the regular speed of the recording. Then he must be able to visualize any corrections or reinforce the strong points in the techniques.

Notes:

_____

_____

_____

_____

_____

_____

_____

_____

•••••••
Staying Ready

Waiting until you get the starting job is to late to get your mind right.

In season conditioning is a critical element in the pursuit of a championship. There is a tendency towards losing the physical and mental conditioning as the season moves toward its end. This should be on the mind of the athlete because there could come a time when you are called upon to go beyond the normal call of duty. If that is the case, then you want to make sure that you have kept up with your conditioning as much as possible. The best time to get the extra work in is in the early part of the week to provide the body with adequate recovery time. Personally, the mornings worked best for me. I would get up at 6 a.m. and ride the bike for 20-25 minutes. Some mornings I would just do an aerobic workout, and other mornings I would do intervals to work on my turnover for speed. Okay, stop laughing! I did have a little speed, but more than likely it was straight up quickness.

This is critical for everyone, but even more so for the players that are not getting enough action on game day. The back-up that will get a couple reps during the week and might get one or two during the game, or the back- up that will get a lot of reps during the week but none on game day really needs to make sure that he is ready. It only takes one occurrence and you could be the guy. So make sure that you get some extra work off the field so when the opportunity arises, you are prepared to be the best of your ability. It will be a change going from not playing to playing, a little to a lot, but that's okay. Be ready!

On the mental side of things, make sure you are keeping up with everything just like you could start the game. Again, this is a tough situation to be in. You must stay focused just like you are the MAN. It is best to be ready and not get the opportunity than as opposed to not being ready and getting the opportunity. If you will, while you are watching the practice tape, imagine that it is you running each play. This will take discipline and imagination, but it is a way to maintain sharpness and remain interested in what is happening. The more you can put those thoughts in your mind, the more likely it will manifest.

Notes:

_____

_____

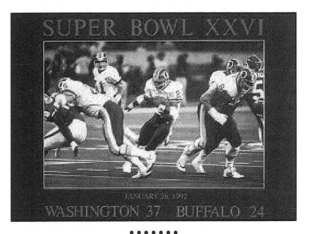

Off Season Workout and Visualization

For me, I believe SBXXVI was a by-product of my off-season training and visualization.

When I was training in Cleveland after the 1989 trade, I would say and think to myself "I am a champion" during my runs. I would say this over and over again, "CHAMPION, CHAMPION." At times I would raise both hands in the air as if I had scored a touchdown. Years later, that image and thought became a reality, and I believe that those words and that image planted in my mind gave me courage to move forward into the unknown. I became that which I thought of most.

It's advantageous for the player to see the results of his off-season training as clearly as possible. Why do I say this? Most players approach and perform off-season conditioning to get in shape. As a matter of fact, all players that workout during the off-season does it for that reason. Some professional athletes might have an incentive clause in their contracts that specifies a certain amount of money if they workout in the club facility. My point here is that most of the guys or people in that position do so just to condition. Most endure the workout without thinking or considering what they are working for. What I am suggesting is that prior to a workout, each player or athlete should consider what's at stake when he or she goes out for the training session. Put in mind what they desire to accomplish through a particular workout. The area that needs to be improved, visualize that area and as the workout continues, keep reminding them of the image. If a player had a problem with catching the ball, visualize yourself catching the ball fluently, following the ball all the way to the hands. Another helpful way to get more out of off-season training is to think and say positive affirmations during the workout. If a player has a lack of confidence, during the workout have him say or think," I am strong and look forward to the challenge that's coming my way."

Notes:

_____

_____

_____

•••••••

Focus Throughout

The 2000 Super Bowl team had the ability to be focused when needed.

The 2000 Baltimore Ravens won the Super Bowl with a large number of veteran players. But there were also some young pups mixed in. The team had a great defense along with a big time return guy by the name of Jermaine Lewis. This team was the most relaxed team that I had ever been around. They laughed and joked during practice, but when it was time for them to go into individual offensive or defensive periods they could turn it on.

I believe that when you are practicing you should be focusing on the task at hand. Talking about what you want to do later or after the game is not a way to get better or to negate mental mistakes. With that said, I believe that you should be able to relax, have fun, and laugh with your co-workers. Know we need to get back to work as soon as possible. Focus and discipline are two keys. Focusing on your job and on the reason that you are on the field is imperative. While focusing, you will realize the importance of what you desire and what you are trying to accomplish.

There are so many obstacles that can affect your ability to focus. One might be a teammate that is not starting. He can't afford to be a distraction, but sometimes he is. When he decided to play around with you as opposed to keeping his attention on the job, he is hurting both himself and the starter. The player that isn't starting actually needs to be more focused than the player that is getting the most repetitions, simply because he is not getting the physical reps and needs to get as many mental reps as possible. If this is the case, you must recognize it and perhaps find a way to discuss it with your teammate. However, first make sure that you take care of your business. The reps at practice as well as the meeting time are too valuable for the proper attention to not be given. Make sure that you know your information so well that it becomes part of you. The analogy is that when you ingest food it becomes you, so when you ingest the game plan, it becomes yours. Thus, it becomes a part of your way of operating.

At times the coach can be a distraction. If he is giving too much information or you haven't taken the time to show that you know what to do, then he will always be shouting instructions at you. If you know the game plan and you can show it but he is constantly in your ear, let him know in a respectful way, "Hey, coach, I got your back" or "I got this." This will more than likely give him peace of mind, especially when you go out and produce.

Side note on FOCUS: If you want to improve during the course of the season, then you should start out focusing on a single part of your game. The choices will vary depending on your position and the level of play that you have attained. Know that you can and should always look for ways to improve. Whether you are a Pro-Bowler or on the practice squad, improvement is a possibility.

Focusing on one thing begins with the recognition that enhancement is needed. Next, implement the process at the beginning of practice and work on that particular area during training. Every chance you get work and focus on the single task and by the end of the week, that part of the game you've wanted to improve will be part of your game. A lot of my best play was at the end of the season or in the playoffs. Additional cardio during the season helped me gain strength.

Each week continue to focus on one thing and continue to work until it becomes part of your game. One of the best ways to continue the growth process is to get back to what you love. Continue to push yourself. Never over-think the ideas.... Keep it simple!!

Reasons to focus on one improvement per week:

1) It gives you something to work on while allowing you to focus on something particular at practice. It's difficult to improve your whole game at once, but if you focus on one part of your game then you will eventually improve your entire game.

2) For young players, focusing on one improvement can provide immediate success, and therefore it can give them confidence.

Notes:

_____

_____

_____

_____

_____

_____

_____

_____

_____

_____

_____

_____

•••••••
Playing a Former Team:
Adjusting Because of Playing Conditions

Cleveland Stadium was full of surprises on GameDay. We had to play in whatever Lake Erie decided to give us..

I had played for the Cleveland Browns for 5 years. We had been in the play-offs 4 of those years. I had a variety of success on an individual level.

As a person, negative plays tend to be the ones that drove me nuts. The countless number of good to great plays was distant in my mind and seemed to be in some of the columnist mind (Esp. Bill Livingston). The plays that cost the city, our fans, the team and me chances at the ultimate success, were the ones that made it essential that I get out of town. When looking for perfection, the negative plays get more attention. I had started to feel the need for change while contemplating retirement. I don't believe I actually told anyone except, perhaps, my agent (Allen Herman). He was able to work with the Redskins and the Browns to get a new contract and a trade done which culminated on draft day.

I knew this was happening but didn't realize the magnitude. I went out to play golf on draft day but couldn't relax. I tried to get away, but for the first time in my golfing career had to walk off of the course. My nerves were all over the place.

There were a number of plays that I wanted do overs on, but they end up being the ones that had begun my exit. I believe the two personal foul penalties I got, against the OILERS in the 1989 play-offs, were a build up of frustration. That never excuses mistakes or errors.

I believe the very next pre-season, I was back in Cleveland wearing another uniform.

Playing a team that you formally played for will be full of an increased level of energy. The focus is keen all week long, even though most of the guys say that it's just another game. There is a feeling that something needs to be proved. When this is the case, it can be easy to get too high for the game. So the player needs to be aware of this and make sure that he can use this energy to play at a higher level instead of going out and trying to do too much. If he can use this increased level of energy, he will be able to play at the level he is accustomed to.

I can remember playing the Browns the year after I was traded to the Redskins. I dressed in that little visitor's locker room. I had the feeling of being in a dream. Even though it was a preseason game, I was pumped up, or geeked as I like to say. One of the coaches (Emmitt Thomas) saw me before the game and said to me, "Earnest, remember this is just a preseason game." I remember smiling but thinking, yeah.... okay.

I scored a touchdown on a run where I was nearly flipped. Afterwards, I started towards the Browns' sideline while yelling and screaming. I don't know what got into me. I was temporarily insane.

Each time a player plays his former team there is something different in the air that particular day. It's special...Period! It's not that you owe them, but you do. For most players you can expect the players best.

Playing Conditions

On game day there are a number of things that can influence the way a player plays the game. The list can include: Lack of sleep the night before, something might have happened to a loved one during the week, he might have a cold or upset stomach. The good ones know how to focus and use the energy to play the game.

By the way, speaking of an upset stomach, I had one of my best games when I played with Washington and we played the Oakland Raiders. I must have had food poisoning because I was throwing up and working the other end too. I was sure I wasn't going to be able to play. Some kind of way I went out for pre- game...made it through that...dang! Then made it through the beginning of the game. Then four quarters later, I had scored three touchdowns and a bunch of catches. It was survival.

Another factor that may influence the way a player plays a game is that he may have an argument with his significant other. I know for sure I had my fair share of arguments with my wife on the way to Redskin games. Luckily, I had the ability to turn my thoughts of disagreement off and focus on the game. When I left the parking lot and entered the locker room the game became the issue. For my wife, being with the other wives must have changed her focus. Most of the time, the argument was forgotten after the game. Go figure. Maybe that was a way my wife decided to get me ready for the game.

Players may also be affected if the weather is inclement. If the weather is an obstacle to any player, then there needs to be recognition of this. I was once told that the conditions that you practice or play in are a part of the day. The focus should be on what you have to do to be successful and not on the weather. When I was at East Carolina Robbie Barrow, my college coach, told me that the weather is just part of the game. I can remember playing little league football while it was sleeting. I stood out on the field with no affects. I was always comfortable no matter what the weather was. For the coaches, we might need to consider what needs adjusting for the player.

When the adjustments have been made, then go out and focus on your game. Players on opposing teams would often complain about the conditions of the Cleveland field after the game. With this being the case, we knew that as the home team we had a mental advantage before the ball was snapped. The opposing team had an excuse for failure. If it is raining or snowing before the game, maybe consider changing you spikes, think about keeping your gloves dry, adjust the way you catch balls –using your body if necessary, or don't wear gloves at all. If the wind is blowing and can change the trajectory of the ball when it is in the air, think of watching the ball even more than you would normally.

If the athlete is thinking about what he can't control, he is obviously looking for reasons not to achieve or ways not to win. Always focus on what is needed to be at the top of your game. Personal victory and defeating your opponent is the objective.

Notes:

• • • • • • •

Football Plagiarism

As a player I watched a number of guys on video. The one I learned the most from was Marcus!

One great learning tool is to watch other players that play the position you play. As a player, I used to watch Emmitt Smith and Marcus Allen. They were players that played a similar game to mine and both played at a high level. Whenever I got the chance to watch those guys perform, I would have my note pad out and my visualization techniques heightened. On one occasion I was watching Marcus pass protect against Johnny Mead, a linebacker from the Houston Oilers, that I was having trouble blocking. From watching Marcus, I actually got the answer I needed to play against Mead. He was a finesse rusher with quickness. Marcus used a fake cut to make the rusher hesitate and then jumped him for a successful block. I started practicing that technique and used it the next week.

To attempt to play the perfect game is an admiral task, but it's one that drives the most dominant and incredibly successful performers. You must look to continue the learning process. I mean, don't ever feel like you have everything figured out. If you do, that's when complacency sets in and quite possibly the inevitable start to decline as a player.

Some players are too proud to use this tool simply because they want to re-create the wheel. Watch the people that are having success in an area that you want to improve so you can decrease the amount of time needed to learn and grow as a player. The quicker you can pick up information and add it to your game the faster you can reach the goals that you have set for yourself.

Use football plagiarism because it's worth it.

Notes:

_____

_____

_____

_____

_____

_____

_____

• • • • • • •

Feeling Your Game

Staying in your zone takes focus on your basics even when playing your best.

In 1999, the Redskins were playing the Cardinals. One thing you must understand regarding this game is that the Redskins had never lost to the Cardinals during that time. However, that's another issue. I was having a game where everything was flowing. I was in the zone. Instead of staying in the zone, I wanted to get fancy and break a play outside when I darn well knew it was an inside run. I would have gotten it, but the defender got his hands on the ball and yep, it came out and he recovered. Okay, I was brought back down to earth without a parachute. It took me out of the flow. I had to regroup and start again. If I had stayed with what I was doing and stayed with the basics, then my flow would have continued. We won the game, but it changed my mentality in regards to the good feeling I had.

Earnest Byner's *Everybody Fumbles*

There are days when everything seems to go your way on a personal level as well as on the team level. How do you keep this going without doing anything that will assist your opponent? The best way to handle this is to recognize that this type of day is happening. The tendency is to just let everything loose and just go with the flow. In football, this can be dangerous because when you relax too much the unexpected has a way of waking you up from your dream and disturbing the flow for a while. To deter anything that will assist the opponent or take you out of your flow, make sure that you stay focused. The flow is nice and the zone that you are in is a very good thing. So make sure that you keep the flow going by taking care of the little things. Stay mentally disciplined enough to take care of the plays that are presented. The big plays will naturally happen.

On the other end of the spectrum is the day when nothing seems to be going right. The best way to handle this situation is to again, recognize that this is happening and be aware of what types of feelings accompany this situation. The way most of us deal with this is negative. The feelings run from disappointment to anger to despair. If you let these feelings set in, you will not be able to concentrate on what is needed. The focus will be on what has happened instead of what you desire. If you get down on yourself and let the feelings set in, it's possible that when the play comes to you or the opportunity is presented for you to make a play, you will miss out. This becomes a double whammy because your negative feelings have perpetuated it. Your lack of concentration may cause you to tumble.

So in each of these situations, make sure that you focus on the basics and do your best to keep emotions in check. If you get too high and caught up in the moment, then you leave yourself open to an incident that can bring you down. If you are too low, then something may happen to take you even lower. Stay in the moment and keep the mental discipline that will help you be successful.

Notes:

_____

_____

_____

_____

_____

• • • • • • •
Game Plans and Strategies

Search for common ground when questions about agendas come up.

What the hell are the coaches thinking about?? They don't know what they are doing. Players make these statements constantly. One thing to keep in mind when there are questions concerning what a coach or someone in the organization decided is that they are in it to win just like you.

There are times when you might see it to the contrary. Never forget that coaches get paid and have jobs based on their performance and even more importantly their WINS. There may be disagreements and personal agendas, but you must realize that the main objective is to win. If you are a coach wanting to get a top job and your team or players are not playing at a high level, do you think that someone else will hire you with this in mind? If this coach gets hired it will possibly be because of another variable, such as acquaintances or a close friend in position to make the call. The same scenario applies to an individual that is in management.

So as a player, if you keep this in mind when you have a disagreement on strategies or purpose, consider the possibilities.

One other situation to avoid is when you recognize an injustice. If you recognize an injustice, don't let it become personal unless it is personal. When you let it become personal, there is a possibility that it can and or will affect your level of commitment and desire to play the game. When recognizing an injustice, take note of it. Learn as much as you can from the situation because the same situation might catch you. One reason you want to take note is if you are not going through it now, you will soon have to deal with something similar.

This very situation changed my career in Cleveland and had me very disenfranchised with the organization. I saw where some guys, in my mind, where being treated unfairly. It bothered me to the hilt. I internalized this and it became personal. It made me not like the game anymore and took away some of the fire and enjoyment I had regarding the game. I had to have a good talk with Earnest Byner, so I could get myself redirected.

The best way to deal with something on this level is to discuss it with someone that has had some exposure concerning the situation. It can be spoken amongst your teammates, but the likelihood is that it will only cause further dissension unless there are level heads within the group. Seek out someone that has experience. Spend some time getting understanding then watch as you grow and expound upon your level of knowledge.

Notes:

_____

_____

_____

_____

_____

_____

_____

_____

_____

_____

_____

_____

_____

_____

• • • • • • •
Taking the Game on Your Shoulders

Always be ready to stand up when times are hard.

There were two, maybe three, situations in my career where I was the goat and made out to be the only one playing the game. One situation was in the season of "The Fumble". We were driving late in the game, Cleveland versus Indy at home and we were in field goal range, which would have tied the game. I was called on a simple gut play and was going down, but I relaxed and fumbled the ball. They recovered and won the game. I had to handle this situation. I had cost the team the opportunity to win. The game has been played and your team has lost. There is one play that stands out in your mind. It's a play that you think has caused the team to lose the game. The reality is that it did cost the team, but it wasn't the only reason for the loss.

So now you are down in the dumps and you feel like you have let everyone else down as well. So many 'what ifs' hit you that you can't even think straight! What do you do when this happens? First of all, recognize the need for blaming someone each time a game is lost. There is a mentality that prevails in our society concerning who done it. We seem to need a bad guy to point our fingers at and a scapegoat must be crucified. Coaches and players are included in this.

You can start by recognizing that your play did contribute to the loss. If you do this, then you have begun the healing process. Own up to what had happened and learn from the event.

Next, realize that if you are on a team then there were other plays in the game and unless everyone else played the perfect game there were other mistakes made. Perfection is what we ascribe to, but it is an illusion. You can try to play the perfect game, but you must be willing and ready to accept the mistakes that will be made. Be willing to grow with them. Be gentle with yourself about your mistakes. We as individuals sometimes have a tendency to be harder on ourselves than others are on us. Now, I don't want you not taking responsibility for you mistakes, as I said before, and I don't want you to be flippant or coy concerning it either. If you come across as being coy, there is an attitude of "I don't care" perceived by others. No one wants to be around an individual who does not care about success, let alone be concerned about the team's welfare. On the other front, no one wants to be around you if you are feeling sorry for yourself either because you will spread your negative energy to others.

Players want others around who truly desire to be great. That mentality can help the individual and the team to reach higher heights.

If you have to do an interview, make sure you own up to your mistakes and make sure that you learn from it. Be honest. Be a guy that will stand up when times are bad so when good times come you will enjoy them all the more. Balance of life dictates that with the bad experience, good will follow and vice versa.

It's okay to be concerned about what you do, but be concerned in a way that produces growth. If you do not grow from bad experiences, you will suffer similar experiences over and over again until you learn. You will be hindered from going to the next level.

Play like the game is in your hands on every play, but be willing to accept less than perfect while you grow with every experience. In reality, the game is in your hands and each play can determine the outcome.

Notes:

_____

_____

_____

_____

· · · · · · ·
Occupational Hazard

Here Bill T. is taking care of me after one of my many occupational hazards.

My second stint in Cleveland was an excellent experience. Mr. Modell welcomed me back with a press conference and the Cleveland fans embraced me without reservation. It was 1994 early in the off-season and Ozzie Newsome had given me a call to test my interest concerning coming back. I told him I would be interested. That gave me some additional motivation to train. So when training camp came that year, I was ready.

I had had a great training camp. Quickness and speed showed up because of the training I had done. My cuts were sharp. But hold up, the hamstring needed a break. Ouch!! It pulled. One day while getting treatment, I caught myself looking at other guys and wondering why they were healthy. I wanted a leg transplant. The occupational hazard got me. There are many events that happen in life to be concerned about. For athletes, one of the main concerns is what I call an occupational hazard. Injuries can affect the obvious, which is the physical ability to perform the task at hand. Injuries can change the way a player will approach the game and how he plays the game. An injury can affect practice time AND WHEN A PLAYER CAN'T PRACTICE, IT INVARIABLY HAMPERS HIS PERFORMANCE.

When I injured my hamstring in Cleveland, I can remember being in the training room. While getting treatment, I would look at the healthy players and wonder about their hamstrings and why they weren't hurt. The questions are usually, 'why me and why now?' So the injury can play mind games with an athlete as well.

Just like making a mistake can put a guy in the tank, so can an injury. The injury will sometimes bring feelings of depression and feelings of not being worth a nickel with a hole in it. The player can feel like he had let the team down and that he is no longer a contributor to the team. There can be a feeling of being disconnected when a player can't participate in practice or the game. When the coach does not check on the player, the player may play more mental games with himself. He will wonder about what the coach is thinking and he may think that the coach only likes him when he can help him. I am not going to tell you when or who, but I can remember a coach stating something very derogatory about a player while he was laying on the field in agony. What the hell was he thinking? Not all coaches are like this, but it is something in the player's mind when he is injured, especially when the coach does not pay him any attention or check on him while injured.

It was 1986 when a defender surprised me and got my foot stuck in the ground. All the ligaments blew up. I can remember feeling very nervous when I attended my first game after ankle surgery. Game day is especially tough when a player is injured. So if you can focus your attention on assisting others with their preparation, you will feel like you are contributing and not be focused on the fact that you are not playing. This will also help you during the week when you can't practice. It is common for the athlete to be isolated when he stays in the training room for treatment. If it is possible, he should be at practice and around the guys, so he can be connected in some way.

One way of feeling better is realizing that there is nothing you can do to change what has happened. The injury has manifested itself and the thing to focus on is what can remedy the situation. The only thoughts you should have should be those that are focused on healing and what is desired when the body is healing. That's right, the body will heal itself! If the individual is worried, mad, disappointed, depressed, or having any other negative thoughts, the body will be affected adversely. The thoughts that you have will permeate the body and affect it in different areas. Just think about it and reflect on any negative thoughts you have had, and you will recognize that your body was affected. So, when you are injured think about getting back on the field and use visualization techniques to continue the healing. Keep in the mind only what you truly desire. It is crucial to keep the mind positive even when negative thoughts want to be present.

When recovering from an injury, it can be a good idea to push to the point of pain. When you reach this point, STOP and put some ice on the injury right away. Placing ice on the injured area will help keep the swelling down and assist in the healing process. You will build yourself back up, so you will have the ability to go a little further the next time you are rehabilitating. Be smart when you have had to take some time off. There will be a tendency to do too much. Be careful. Even though you might feel good, don't over-do it. Build yourself up on a steady and consistent pace.

When you are lifting or moving the injured part, make sure that you locate and feel the naturalness of the uninjured counterpart of the body. Feel that strength and recognize that there is no pain. When you do this, this thought then transfers to the part of the body that needs healing. While you are doing this, imagine yourself doing the skill that you desire. It might be that you have to remember a place or time prior to the injury. You might have to get some old film and look at it to plant the vision that is needed. When you do this, the thoughts and feelings associated will be transferred to the whole body, especially the area that needs healing. It might take special attention for the injured part, but make sure all your thoughts are in the affirmative manner.

Notes:

_____

_____

Number One Versus Number Two

Having a good competition at the same position can help drive the individuals and the team to a higher level.

This situation happened to me when the Cleveland Browns drafted Allen in the first round from Florida State University. The comments during the off-season about the running back position concerned the need for speed. No one in our backfield had blazing break way speed at the time, including yours truly. So we drafted someone that was supposed to fill that void. Now, my question is where is this guy going to get the reps needed to help us? There was Kevin Mack, Herman Fontenot, and myself already in the rotation. Obviously this guy was drafted to sit the bench. WRONG!! What was the only thing left for me to do? I sat around, moped, and just let the guy come in and have my job. Wrong again. I decided that I would work to improve my speed and be in the best shape of my career going into training camp. The challenge was issued prior to the draft with the conversation around the need for speed and it was solidified for me when the draft choice was made. I knew what I had to do, and I knew that I wanted to continue to be the man and contribute at a high level.

Challenges have a way of rising up at different times throughout one's career. Whether during practice or a game, one player can surface that has the potential to be a contributor on the team. If the player is not a starter, he may have the potential of replacing the guy in front of him. When this happens and it is handled in the appropriate way, the number one guy can be pushed to higher heights, which in turn will make the team better. Take the challenge as something positive. The requirements of the position and the development of your skills will heighten your awareness and focus. Every day is the day to win the battle. For me, it became personal. I wanted to be the man while keeping the other person in my rearview mirror. I wanted to take every rep, so I could make sure that I was prepared for every situation. By doing that, I kept the number two guy in his place. While I recognized the threat, I continued also to stay focused on my own motives and game.

One might see this as a threat and become overly consumed with the possibility of being replaced. If that is the case, then the player will be taken out of his game. He will be thinking about the 'what ifs' and not be focused on what the immediate task requires. There is a possibility that the individual could lose confidence in this situation and start to look for some answers outside of self. A person that has been in this position can make a difference on your team. With the recognition of the situation he can keep the number one guy properly motivated and directed.

As a coach, I will use this situation to drive each player to higher heights. I know from experience that each player will watch to see what the other one does. They use this as a form of motivation. This type of competition is one that can, if used properly, push the team to higher heights. My idea is to challenge each guy by asking them in front of each other what it is that he wants. I will ask the number two, three, and four guys if they want the number one spot. If the player hedges, then you know you don't want him on the team. But when they speak the truth and state, yes, they want it, then you have the situation that you want at that position. We keep it honest and open without any bad vibes. Everybody knows how the others feel about playing, so the competition is on. If you handle the situation this way, all possible obstacles are avoided and each player can go on to support the other while pushing each other to higher heights.

I went on to have a good year while competing against someone that wanted my job. Kevin Mack and I were the best of friends at the time, but we kept each other motivated with little challenges here and there. He was a star at the time and so was I. I wanted the ball and so did he. This didn't interfere with what we were trying to accomplish as a team. It drove us to the playoffs and kept the team moving ahead.

Number one vs. number two is a good thing for the position and team if you have the right type of players and a coach that knows what he is doing.

If the coach can't handle this or if you have some players who look at this the wrong way, then you have a potentially cancerous situation.

Notes:

_____

_____

_____

_____

_____

_____

_____

_____

272	Denver Broncos	Bobby Micho	Tight end	Texas
273	Detroit Lions	James Thaxton	Defensive back	Louisiana Tech
274	Los Angeles Rams	Joe Dooley	Center	Ohio State
275	San Francisco 49ers	Dave Moritz	Wide receiver	Iowa
276	Pittsburgh Steelers	Kirk McJunkin	Tackle	Texas
277	Miami Dolphins	John Chesley	Tight end	Oklahoma State
278	Dallas Cowboys	Brian Salonen	Tight end	Montana
279	Washington Redskins	Keith Griffin	Running back	Miami (FL)
280	Cleveland Browns	Earnest Byner	Running back	East Carolina

• • • • • • •

The Uncertainty of the Draft

Drafted the last player in the 10th round by the Browns didn't give me any uncertainty.

It was day two of the 1985 NFL draft. I was sitting in a dorm room waiting to see if the phone would ring. I can remember saying that I just wanted to be drafted so I can get a signing bonus. The phone rang late that day. It was the tenth round and I spoke to then Head Coach Sam Ritigliano and Mr. Modell. I could go home and let my wife know the good news. What round am I going to be drafted in? What if I don't get drafted?

Should I come out early? There are so many uncertainties that a college player goes through until the moment that his name is called and the phone call with the owner, general manager, and head coach has taken place.

Turn this around a bit. The player already in the league has to be dealing with the 'what ifs' also. He had played one, two, three, or more years. His position is always under scrutiny and there is a pressure that comes with the draft. One might be heard saying, "Man, they don't need to draft a back. I can carry the load if they just give me the chance." The first round or two go by and they don't draft anyone at my position. GREAT! I am okay once again. There is a sense of relief that comes to the player and those that are closest to him. As far as he is concerned, this is a personal attack.

Let's say that this does happen in the opposite format. They do draft someone, and he is heralded as the next savior. He will be someone that will take this team, my team, to the next level. A question may be, "Am I as good as I thought?" Self-doubt becomes a part of the player at this time. He may start to look at all the things that are being said about this savior. Is he offended or does he feel slighted? You're damn right!! The trouble is that once a team gets the one they think will take them to the promise land, they seem to forget the one that they have alienated. The one person that has been the source of dependency for the team up until this point is pushed to the side. The player should have some reassurance about his position on the team or given some parameters in consideration of the job he will be asked to do. We all need pats on the back sometimes.

This should be noted.

Let's get back to the thoughts of the player already on the team. He is wondering about his teammates. What are they thinking? The struggle is on. Where can he find solace? The only way he can and will find refuge is to get on with his own preparation. At this point there is and will be some doubts associated. There is still a feeling of being inadequate and a lack of confidence based on these feelings. Stress is an everyday form of life in this game and comfort is not a necessary part of life. To be honest, the challenge has already been there prior to anyone else coming into the mix.

Problems that can come out of this situation can include self-abuse, some sort of mate abuse, loss of confidence, and a feeling that some form of stature has been taken away. There is a tendency to point the finger at other people. The question becomes "what does he have that I don't?" Thinking of taking his game to the next level has to be his modus operandi. Strength of character and perseverance of the player being challenged is a huge key. How determined are you? Setting your goal is even more important at this time. If you have goals set, review them and get a fresh picture in your mind. Become more adamant about what you want instead of regulating yourself to do something less. Self-inventory is important. What are my strengths and weaknesses? What can I control and what should be my focus?

Notes:

_____

_____

_____

_____

_____

_____

_____

_____

_____

_____

_____

_____

_____

_____

_____

_____

· · · · · · ·
Blogs

Leaders must have the strength to stand up to and challenge those that have self-serving desires. They have the ability to stand in and up for those with less leadership ability. Understanding that the influence that they have been given is ultimately a gift. There will be times when they must make the vision clear so the team can succeed.

Trials will come to the organization just as each individual. Life provides experiences that prepare us for the next phase. Rarely does anything come out of the blue. Reflection will give indicators.

When a challenge comes that threaten the many and will ultimately cause loss, those that are leaders are called upon to make it right. Those leaders must be ones cut from a different cloth. While being understanding, they should have empathy and wisdom.

Having the ability to bring negative thoughts and actions into "oneness" will galvanize the team.

Notes:

_____

_____

_____

_____

_____

_____

_____

_____

_____

_____

_____

_____

• • • • • • •

Position Coaches and Individual Time

One of the most important things a position coach needs is individual time with his players.

Position coaches are golden jobs in the league. Some people lose jobs for no apparent reason and are out. Some will be looking but can't find one.

Oh snap that's me. Yeah EB they are to be cherished. Dang I digress! Back to the story at hand. Each position needs, wants and craves individual meeting and training time.

The meeting time avails a coach the opportunity to detail the assignments, to show video of the plays, so they see how the play looks when ran correctly, to go over adjustments and to ask and answer questions.

The individual training time gives opportunity to work on a lot of basic football mechanics and technique, which will fortify their foundation. This all builds up to how efficient they play on game day.

If they don't get that individual time, they have to be crafty with getting the daily details and technical instructions. For a lost individual will cost the team the loss of a game.

Come hell or high cotton, he will get that time because he cares about the players performance and does not desire the play to be messy because of his player... it's his ash. A lot of the time it's a delicate balance based on the philosophy of the offensive coordinator. The ones I was in the den with delivered for me (except one). So it gave me the opportunity to really get down and teach.

I loved it!!! Even with some of the challenges I had. But that's another story.

Notes:

_____

_____

_____

_____

_____

_____

_____

• • • • • • •
Deadly Serious/Raise the Level

""I learn just from watching him, the way he practices and prepares. During games, he is always giving me suggestions and tips about reads and other things to look for." Jay Graham

Giving all I had mentally, physically and emotionally was the way I've always done everything. Each practice, meeting, workout or drills in practice were all meant to be done all out with the correct technique and motive.

Ray Ellis came to Cleveland in mid-season with a rep of being a tough, hard nose player. I watched him some in practice to see what he would do and how he was practicing. For some reason, I didn't like it that he was supposed to be tough. So once I got a chance during a play, I blocked him then went on to push him after the play and stand jump into his chest. My energy wanted him to know how we worked during that time and that all we did out there on the field was to be all out. We came to respect each other and cheered each other on.

We were in south Florida (Vero Beach) preparing for our play-off game vs the Dolphins. We were in our 9 on 7 run drill. We were beating each other up, but because it was the play-offs, I was going especially hard because it was do or die. Because of the intensity, the drill was stopped. We were getting ready with the thought of the game in mind. That made us sharper and more focused. We went on to play Miami down to the wire, but ended up losing However, we played at a high level, which gave us confidence for the next season.

It was the end of the 91 season, and we (Redskins) were in Minnesota getting ready for the Super Bowl. We always practiced in pads. But this Friday, we practiced in nothing but helmets. This decision was made on Wednesday when during practice you could hear the crispness of practice. The level again had been raised at practice because of the game we were preparing for. Joe and the staff didn't want us to kill each other. We went on to dominate the Bills and from my perspective, it all started at Wednesday practice.

Practice for me was always serious. There wasn't time for me to be jovial, tell jokes or be out of focus. Preparation and how an individual and team look are critical to success on game day.

Notes:

_____

_____

_____

_____

_____

_____

_____

_____

_____

_____

_____

••••••

Basics

Off to another good start vs the Cardinals! But wait...
Get back to your basics!

It's a beautiful fall day. Sunday at RFK Stadium in Washington DC was always magical feeling. It's a divisional game, so we gotta have it today. We have a good feel about it because we don't lose to these guys (Cardinals). It's what some call a stat game.

I'm on a roll because it's been one hundred yard game after the next; I'm in the zone. The one we talk about where everything slows down. Yea...I'm in it.

It's about mid-way through the second quarter and I'm off to another good start. I'm warm, so I got a nice lather, i.e...sweat is pouring, but I'm good.

Coach Joe Gibbs calls one of our favorite plays. 40 Gut. Remember I'm feeling it and rolling to another one hundred yard game. I get to my alignment, take my customary pre-snap read, locate my first read as Ryp (Mark Rypien) is calling out the snap count, and BAM... the ball is snapped. The play calls for specific footwork. I push off and start to open cross over and get downhill between the guard and the tackle. I'm consistent, so I do it while I'm still eying my first read. I feel some leakage from my right, so I bounce it outside. No problem, but dang the ball slips out of my hand and they recover. Momentum Killer! Reality check for me. Ok. I'm on the sideline going back over the play. I'm good with handling the ball. Protecting it has been a huge requirement with Coach Gibbs. I feel why I got caught this time. I had gotten a little cocky and let the ball get away from me so, the defender, while trying to grab me, tipped the ball. I got my lesson.

Part of my lesson had to do with staying focused on my basics when I'm in a grove. When good things are happening, the basics have been mastered, but they must always be reinforced. Maybe better said, "Don't get the big head".

I changed gloves because, if you remember, I was sweaty due to me rolling in sand-it was a warm day. As customary, Joe comes back to me with my fresh gloves and renewed motivation. But wait what's this feeling? The ball feels different and there is a more assuring feeling.

The combination of the new gloves and me already sweating made it feel even stickier. This lead me to change gloves after I got sweaty instead of waiting for the ball to slip out of my hands and kill what we were already building. It was a valuable lesson as we progressed to another Redskin Super Bowl.

Notes:

_____

_____

_____

_____

_____

_____

_____

_____

_____

· · · · · · ·

Roles

Going against guys like Clay Mathews got me ready to roll in my starting role later in 1984.

So we have gotten through the 1984 marathon called training camp. We really played a full season when you consider the amount of 2 a day practices with pads.

Now it's time to start preparing for the season and individual games. When you prepare for an opponent there have to be guys on the team who play the role of the other team. We call them scrubs...LOL...just kidding. They are the look team, also known as the scout team. I like to use the phrase opportunity unit. To me, it's a chance to show what you can do. It's a role that should be cherished.

They service the first and second team guys, so they have an idea what they will be facing on game day. Most of the time, especially now, the scout team is little more than a walk through mentality or tempo. Because of the salary cap, the guys with big money contracts and those that have regular contracts can't be injured. It may cost someone a job sooner than later. The team can't afford it. To me, this takes away some of the potential development of the starters and the guy who's role it is to give the look.

How sharp can you really be when you really don't get to go full speed when practicing? As the season goes, the occupational hazard called injuries will happen. Has the developmental guy that's now needed in the starters role truly gotten ready? I digress.

When fall 1984 rolled around, it was my job to get the starting defense ready. I was the runner and often played a receiver when needed. But the one job I enjoyed most was playing fullback. I had a chance to hone my skills and go against guys like Clay Mathews, Eddie Johnson, Chip Banks and Tom Cousaneau. It was a battle every week. It got me ready to face Reggie McKenzie (Raiders), Al Wilson (Oilers), Reggie Williams (Bengals), and Big Lavon Kirkland (Steelers). There was no complaining about going too hard or saving it for the game. Iron and iron going against each other. (Dang hard heads)

Those roles set me up for what was to come later. My approach to that role caught the eyes of the defensive coaches. The main guy was Marty Schottenheimer whom later became the head coach of the Browns. Soon after he had me visit his office? There he told me I was his guy.

I'm convinced that a large part of that decision was made when I played the role of scout team player. If I hadn't done that job the way it was supposed to, then my role may have been to exit the NFL in short time.

Roles have a tendency to change as the season goes on. The guy that you see that's not even dressing for the game may very well be the guy that you are cheering for at the end of the season. Hope that he goes into the year having the vision or given the vision by his coach of preparedness.

Hey, IT COULD!

Notes:

_____

_____

_____

_____

_____

_____

_____

_____

_____

_____

_____

•••••••
Special

Greg Pruitt was one of my predecessors and mentors. He was one of the players in the room in 1984 when I made the team.

It's the night before the final cuts of the 1984 NFL training camp (REAL TRAINING CAMP) Cleveland Browns. Training camp started the weekend after July 4th and lasted for almost two months. It was like being stuck in the twilight zone!

I've been balling from the beginning, so I haven't had an uneasy feeling about being cut. But tonight is a little different. I slept well after I finally fell asleep while half expecting a knock on the door. My roommate has been gone for a week so I'm alone.

I wake up to sunshine and no knock. I pop up and run to the door to take a peek out. QUIET. It was almost spooky. I call home to tell Granny and then call my wife. I made it!

After the call I sat for a while to let it all sink in.

We have a team meeting at 9:00 am. I take what has become my normal seat. Mike Pruitt, Boyce Green, Charles White and Johnny Davis are the other backs. Marty is talking, but I'm in amazement now because

I'm on the team with guys I've watched on TV.

The room is half empty so Marty Schottenheimer's voice almost echoes. But once we get on the field... Wait! Where are the lines of guys waiting to get reps? This is it?! What a realization of how special it is to be on the roster and in the NFL.

Sometimes it's easy to get caught up on the game and the games played that you forget the specialness of being in the league.
Seeing those empty seats and short lines provided an "oh snap" moment for me. Love what you do and Appreciate the constant challenge.

Notes:

_____

_____

_____

_____

_____

_____

_____

_____

• • • • • • •

Respect

Getting your players to buy into your vision is one of the challenges that a coach has. The need to sell them on how you see the team winning comes down to respect at times.

I took what the coaches said to me with unabashed discipleship. My eyes were riveted on the coaches as they spoke to the team. Convinced they had all the answers. I then would be about spreading the word to all the other players myself. As a coach, that's the type of player you want. I know that's the type I would always assume that I had. It got me into trouble sometimes (Digression).

I was a trusting player until I had a coach lie to me about something that made no sense. That made me weak emotionally for a while. I looked at him differently for a while afterwards. For some reason, I felt I couldn't trust him or the game anymore. I continued playing and was blessed to achieve on a high level, but my relationship with the rest of my coaches was affected.

That particular situation also made me coach the way I did. You see... being a consistent coach is the best way to get and keep your players respect.

Players hate coaches that are inconsistent with them and hate more a coach that lies. I worked with a coach that thought he was smarter than everyone else. He thought we were all gullible and just took what he said as the gospel. He didn't have an idea that we knew what he was doing. It affected how guys came to work and how they did their jobs.

On the other hand, when there is a coach that does his best to tell you the truth and if he can't, he will tell you I can't say anything. He has the player's ear and will eventually get to their hearts.

Getting your players to buy into your vision is one of the challenges that a coach has. The need to sell them on how you see the team winning comes down to respect at times. Be consistent with your players and check to see how much further you can get towards your dream.

Notes:

_____

_____

_____

_____

_____

_____

_____

_____

_____

• • • • • • •
Need for a Sports Psychologist

There are a number of reasons for the need for a sports psychologist. The main reason for having one available for the players should be their overall welfare. It's not about being psychoanalyzed. It is about trying to be the best you can be. It is my opinion that all players should meet with a sports psychologist.

The occupational hazard for athletes is injury. When dealing with an injury, an athlete might think less of himself. He will probably have anxieties concerning his job security, his career, or its impeding end and what the coaches and staff think. He might also wonder what his teammates think of him and how they are going to relate to him. When he can't perform the skills that came so naturally to him in the past, there could be pending stress or anxiety.

With this being the case and with the necessity for the player to be of good cheer and have a positive outlook while he is healing, there needs to be someone that has dealt with these types of challenges before. Someone that can assist the player in the acceptance and the adjustments that are necessary for him to get back on the field. This healing process will help him contribute to the team once again. In addition, the psychologist can assist with keeping players balanced in their personal life.

When a player loses his job there is a double-sided coin. The player that is elevated to the starting position is elated and if he is worth what the organization thinks he is worth, then he will respond to the challenge with a higher level of concentration, desire and performance. This player might need to be consulted as to what he is dealing with, along with the player that is being downgraded to a lesser contributor. Doubt, fear, and trust in self and others are affected. Career endangerment, relationships with other teammates, coaches, and families are affected as well.

To assist with the transition and the pending adjustment, there needs to be consideration of what the player will and has experienced. The quicker the player can make a positive move and have a degree of understanding as far as what his future holds, the quicker he can be of assistance to the success of the team.

It is my opinion that someone independent, like a sports psychologist, can help with the transitions in connection with all aspects of life.

• • • • • • •
Conclusion

My desire and hope is that you have been able to make life associations between the short stories shared and your life. Even if the stories do not apply to you or someone associated to you today, they will at some point have an application. My overall intent is to share, teach and enhance lives.
LOVE

Additional *Notes:*

_____

_____

_____

_____

_____

_____

_____

_____

_____

_____

_____

_____

_____

_____

_____

_____

_____

_____

_____

This is the field I first practiced and played on when I began organized football. The hill is what I went back home to run each year.